Why You Should Date Your Bank, Not Marry Them!

Why You Should

Date Your Bank,

Not Marry Them!

Your guide to understanding the mortgage
world and improving your financial confidence

Cara Julian

Illustrations by Sarah Darby
Photography by Mrs Smart Photography
Typesetting by BookPOD

ISBN: 978-1-7636576-0-1 (paperback) 978-1-7636576-1-8 (e-book)

NATIONAL
LIBRARY
OF AUSTRALIA

A catalogue record for this
book is available from the
National Library of Australia

To my daughter Poppy,
for your unwavering support, inspiration
and making me smile every day.
I love you to the moon and back x

Contents

Introduction: Are you settling for less?   1

Chapter 1:   It's time to rewrite your financial story   17

Chapter 2:   Financial foundations   31

Chapter 3:   Demystifying the world of mortgages   63

Chapter 4:   A guide to purchasing and refinancing   85

Chapter 5:   Preparing to partner with a new bank   121

Chapter 6:   Tips and tricks for your mortgage   143

Chapter 7:   Happily ever after   165

Conclusion: Date, don't marry   201

About the author   209

Are you settling for less?

Banking relationships are a lot like romantic relationships. Why should we cling to traditions or practices that no longer serve us or are hopelessly outdated?

There's a prevailing notion that you need to show unwavering loyalty to a single bank for life. You're familiar with it – the bank where you opened your first account, acquired your initial credit card, and diligently put your first earnings. There's a comforting sense of nostalgia and allegiance associated with that institution, but true loyalty should be a two-way street, shouldn't it?

Unfortunately, the banks often fall short in this regard, especially in the context of mortgages. We've all witnessed banks enticing new customers with attractive rates, leaving existing customers in the lurch. Have you ever taken a moment to compare your 'loyal customer' rate with the advertised rates for new customers? It's widely acknowledged in the mortgage realm that there exists a disparity between these rates … and it rarely favours the existing customer (you)! Furthermore, the extended wait times on phone calls, particularly as many bank branches shut, limit face-to-face interactions and further complicate matters.

Is your current bank truly serving your best interests?

It begs the question: Is your current bank truly serving your best interests?

Here's a quick snapshot of the evolving trends in the Australian mortgage market and the impact on customers:

- Innovative marketing strategies: Clever marketing is used to create a perception of loyalty, but banks aren't obliged to operate under 'Best Interest Duty' and act in your best interests.

- Competitive new customer rates: A trend in the market is the offering of more competitive interest rates for new customers, creating an incentive for individuals to switch banks or choose a particular bank.

- Challenges in rate negotiations: Another notable trend is the reluctance of banks to negotiate more competitive rates for existing customers, indicating a shift in focus towards attracting new customers rather than retaining existing ones.

As a mortgage broker, I witness disparity in rates day in and day out. Time and again, I see customers discovering that the rates offered to new customers, or the rates offered by other lenders, are far more competitive than what their bank is offering them. When clients come to me seeking to refinance, I always encourage them to first approach their current bank and try to negotiate a more competitive rate. After all, it's often simpler to stick with what you know, right?

But more often than not, the outcome is disappointing. There's little to no room for movement on the rate. That is, until the eleventh hour of the refinance process. Suddenly, after weeks of the customer's time and effort, after formal approval has been granted and the lender has received the mortgage discharge authority, the retention team swoops in with a last-ditch effort to keep the customer on board. It's baffling, really. Why wait until the customer is on the brink of leaving before offering a reduced rate?

And so the phrase 'You should date your bank, not marry them' was born. It's a call to action. A reminder to keep your options open, keep it casual with your bank, be proactive in your mortgage management and explore what else is out there, and be willing to move on if an offer in your best interests presents itself elsewhere. After all, the banks rake in billions in profit each year. Why not keep some of that in your own pocket?

As you navigate the world of mortgages and financial institutions, remember: loyalty should be a two-way street. Don't hesitate to shop around, negotiate, and demand what you deserve. Your financial well-being is too important to settle for anything less. This is true for everyone. But as you'll discover in this book, I believe it's especially true for women.

As you navigate the world of mortgages and financial institutions, remember: loyalty should be a two-way street.

Empowering women on their financial journey

This book is dedicated to empowering women on their financial journey, particularly in navigating the complex world of mortgages. I'm Cara, a mortgage broker with a passion for supporting women through the mortgage process with financial confidence and bravado.

Why? Because I see a world where women have the confidence to make a change. To challenge the status quo, take control of their finances, and navigate the property market to secure their financial future.

My big game is to create change by championing gender equality in the financial world so we can start the race - all on the same starting line!

I didn't write this book because I had an abundance of spare time; I wrote it because I've experienced firsthand how a lack of financial knowledge and holding on to an outdated mindset can profoundly impact confidence, especially in the seemingly intimidating realm of mortgages.

Like many people, I grew up in an era when traditional gender roles often dictated that men handled the finances in relationships and families.

Throughout my twenties, I struggled to manage my finances effectively. I maintained a rudimentary system made up of a spending account and a nominal savings account, yet invariably found myself living pay cheque to pay cheque.

Like many people, I grew up in an era when traditional gender roles often dictated that men handled the finances in relationships and families. Consequently, this perspective became deeply entrenched in my psyche from an early age.

My journey into the realm of financial responsibility began at the age of sixteen when I entered the workforce. However, despite earning an income, I found myself succumbing to impulsive spending habits, depleting whatever funds I had in my bank account. Upon entering university, I was fortunate enough to have my parents cover my tuition fees. Nonetheless, this did not deter me from acquiring a student loan, not for educational expenses, but rather to fuel my spending habits.

Throughout my twenties, I struggled to manage my finances effectively. I maintained a rudimentary system made up of a spending account and a nominal savings account, yet invariably found myself living pay cheque to pay cheque. Despite my attempts to save by transferring funds into my savings account each month, I inevitably depleted these reserves by month's end.

Consequently, when I married, I defaulted to handing over the reins of financial management to my spouse. Unfortunately (or fortunately depending on the way you look at it!), that marriage didn't last long. But because I had no major financial responsibilities (we sold our property) or debt, and was still young, I just slipped back into my old ways of managing my finances.

I repeated this pattern in my next relationship, abdicating financial responsibility once again. As the years passed and I got older, the importance of making informed financial decisions to secure my future became increasingly apparent. However, I continued to delegate this responsibility to my partner, all while grappling with a lack of financial confidence and independence.

We had a daughter together and I was a stay-at-home mum for six years. Not wanting to re-enter the workforce, I decided to start my own marketing business, which unfortunately failed due to the COVID-19 pandemic.

Ten years later, with a young daughter, no income, and still a low level of financial confidence, the relationship ended. I found myself in a precarious financial position, overwhelmed by uncertainty about the future.

As the years passed and I got older, the importance of making informed financial decisions to secure my future became increasingly apparent.

I was scared and alone, with the weight of the need for financial security on my shoulders. I felt financially vulnerable. I had no game plan. I didn't even know how to take the first step. Despite my apprehension, I recognised the need for change and resolved to take control of my financial destiny. But this process didn't happen overnight. I spent way too long paralysed by fear, unable to navigate my way out!

> Encouraged by a close family friend, and motivated by a desire for financial autonomy, I embarked on a journey of reinvention.

Encouraged by a close family friend, and motivated by a desire for financial autonomy, I embarked on a journey of reinvention. Embracing the opportunity to expand my knowledge and skills, I pursued training to become a mortgage broker, a decision that not only offered financial stability but also gave me the ability to support other women facing similar challenges.

Through my experiences and newfound expertise, I founded Brava Finance with a mission to empower women to take control of their financial futures. By sharing my story and offering guidance, I endeavour to challenge outdated norms regarding money management, foster financial equality, and enable women to navigate the complexities of the property market with confidence.

In essence, Brava Finance represents my commitment to creating a world where women are equipped with the knowledge and resources to build lasting financial security and independence.

Your '101 of mortgages'

My journey to financial security was a winding, pothole-filled road, but it doesn't have to be that way for you. Through my role as a mortgage broker and in this book, I aim to turn my story into your survival guide, providing support, knowledge, and a roadmap to help shift your mindset from overwhelmed and vulnerable to confident and empowered.

Throughout these pages, you'll be challenged to question your truths, disrupt outdated views, and envision a world where you're brave enough to make a change. The mortgage landscape can be daunting, but, by the end of this book, my goal is for you to feel less overwhelmed, armed with the knowledge and motivation to take those crucial first steps towards financial stability.

This book is your '101 of mortgages', covering everything from the basics to the intricacies of home and investment loans, refinancing, and the role of a mortgage broker as your 'wing(wo)man'. Additionally, I'll go through some of the costs involved, as well as common pitfalls to watch out for. Finally, I'll share a series of 'happily ever after' stories of women who have taken control and built a financially secure future for themselves.

So, settle in with your favourite beverage, whether it's a glass of wine or a comforting cup of tea, and get ready to embark on this journey together. Let's build financial confidence, one step at a time.

Are you ready? Let's do this together!

Cara xx

Be Brave | Show Up | Have Fun!

CHAPTER 1

It's time to rewrite your financial story

A brighter future for yourself

Status quo: The existing state of affairs. The current state of social structure, norms or values.

For many women, myself included, the notion that men are the designated caretakers of finances within relationships and families was deeply ingrained from a young age. We observed our fathers, our friends' fathers, and the media all perpetuating this societal norm. Consequently, it became the status quo for many of us.

But here's the thing: it doesn't have to stay that way. My challenge to you is to disrupt this status quo and start breaking down the barriers.

In today's society, it is crucial for women to disrupt the status quo and work towards closing the gender finance gap to ensure economic equality and empowerment. Historically, women have faced barriers in accessing financial resources and opportunities, leading to a significant disparity in wealth accumulation and financial security compared with men. By challenging these norms, it may help women secure their financial independence, potentially making it possible to pursue personal and professional goals without constraints. This not only benefits individual women, but also contributes to a more balanced and equitable economic landscape.

Disrupting the status quo begins with a fundamental shift in mindset.

Disrupting the status quo begins with a fundamental shift in mindset.

Start by questioning why you've accepted this as your reality. Reflect on whether it has truly served you well, or if it's simply what you've been conditioned to believe. Challenge its place in your life and your relationships.

Whether you're in a relationship where your partner manages the finances or you find yourself navigating financial matters solo, it's never too late to make a change.

If you're in a relationship, you can take proactive steps to educate yourself about your financial position. As you'll discover in the next chapter, you can gain a better understanding of your financial goals and strategies. It's time to find your voice and actively participate in decisions that impact your financial future.

If you're on your own, whether due to a recent separation or other circumstances, I commend you for taking the initiative to seek knowledge and empowerment by picking up this book. The next step is to absorb the information within these pages. Arm yourself with the knowledge and confidence needed to take control of your financial situation with bravado and effect change.

I won't sugarcoat it – it won't always be easy. There will be days when it feels like you're taking steps backwards rather than forwards. But remember, it's a journey that requires hard work, dedication and unwavering commitment. And on those tough days, know that you're not alone. You can reach out for support, lean on your community, and keep moving forwards. You have the power to rewrite your financial narrative and create a brighter, more empowered future for yourself.

To quote Rachel Cruze, personal finance expert and bestselling author, 'Financial success is not determined by your circumstances, but by your mindset and actions.'

There will be days when it
feels like you're taking steps
backwards rather than forwards.
But remember, it's a journey that
requires hard work, dedication
and unwavering commitment.

A more equitable financial landscape

Gender gap: An undesirable or unfair difference between men and women in terms of opportunities, pay, status, etc.

In addition to the societal norms we've inherited, women face another challenge in the form of the gender gap, particularly in relation to finance. For example, if children became part of your story, the decision to take time off to give birth and raise them, perhaps as a stay-at-home mum, often leads to a hiatus from the workforce. The longer this period stretches, the more distant you may become from the professional world and opportunities for career advancement, widening the gender finance gap.

During this time, your confidence level may plummet, along with your potential to earn a substantial income. I experienced this firsthand. As I stepped away from the workforce to become a stay-at-home mum (a decision I don't regret for a second!), I not only lost the opportunity to contribute to my superannuation but also found my financial knowledge and confidence dwindling (even further!). I became heavily reliant on my partner for financial support, feeling ill-equipped to navigate the complexities of managing my own finances.

This scenario is all too familiar for many women who have faced similar circumstances. The gender finance gap not only reflects disparities in earnings and financial independence, but also highlights the broader systemic issues that perpetuate gender inequality. It's a multifaceted issue that demands attention and action at both individual and societal levels.

Working towards closing the gender finance gap empowers women to take control of their financial futures, fostering a sense of confidence and self-reliance. Financial literacy and independence are essential tools that enable women to make informed decisions about their investments, savings and spendings.

Working towards closing the gender finance gap empowers women to take control of their financial futures, fostering a sense of confidence and self-reliance.

This knowledge helps equip women in navigating life's challenges, whether it's negotiating salaries, managing

Financially empowered women
are more often than not better
positioned to support their
families and communities,
creating a ripple effect of
positive change and stability.

debt or planning for retirement. Additionally, financially empowered women are more often than not better positioned to support their families and communities, creating a ripple effect of positive change and stability.

It also promotes broader societal benefits, including economic growth and innovation. When women have equal access to financial resources and opportunities, they can contribute more effectively to the economy, driving entrepreneurship and diverse perspectives in business and industry. This inclusivity leads to more robust and resilient economic systems. Encouraging women to disrupt the financial status quo not only champions gender equality, but also helps enable a more dynamic and prosperous future for everyone. By breaking down financial barriers, women can pave the way for a new era of economic inclusivity and shared success.

But here's the silver lining: awareness is the first step towards progress. By recognising the existence of the gender finance gap and acknowledging its impact on your life, you can begin to take proactive steps to address it.

It's about challenging outdated norms, advocating for change, and empowering women to take control of their

> Together, we can pave the way towards a more equitable and inclusive financial landscape for all.

financial futures. And while the journey may be daunting, know that you're not alone. Together, we can pave the way towards a more equitable and inclusive financial landscape for all.

Concerned and vulnerable vs confident and secure

In the next chapter, I outline a step-by-step game plan to help boost your financial confidence and know-how. But first, let's take stock of how you might be feeling about your financial future right now. Perhaps you're:

- **Feeling alone and unsupported:** Feeling isolated and overwhelmed in navigating your financial journey? It's common to feel uncertain and unsupported, unsure of where to begin and who to trust. You wish for guidance and a solid game plan to take those crucial first steps towards financial security. Let's embark on this journey together, empowering you with the knowledge and support to help you thrive financially.

- **Feeling stuck in an old-school mindset:** Feeling trapped by an old-school mindset, which dictates that financial responsibilities are solely for men, can hinder your journey towards financial confidence. If you've been conditioned to believe this narrative and have consequently delegated financial management to your partner, breaking free from this cycle is essential. Let's challenge these outdated norms together, and empower you to take control of your finances and rewrite your financial story.

- **Feeling low in confidence:** Struggling with low confidence and feeling financially vulnerable can create a significant barrier to taking the first steps towards securing your financial future. The constant internal battle with fear and overwhelm often leads to inertia, making it difficult to break free from the cycle. Yet, acknowledging these feelings is the first step towards empowerment. Together, we'll navigate through these challenges, building your confidence and equipping you with the tools to overcome financial obstacles and pave the way towards a more secure future.

Rather than feel concerned and vulnerable, I want you to feel confident and secure about your financial future. That's my goal in this book. Specifically, I aim to help you:

- **Feel supported:** With a guide by your side showing you the way, you'll find yourself more in command of your finances and future. You'll receive the tools and support needed to work towards your financial goals.

- **Boost your confidence:** With a more positive internal dialogue and a reduction in overwhelm, you are more inclined to cultivate a mindset of 'I've got this'. Feelings of financial vulnerability may start to diminish as you gain a stronger sense of control over your finances, leading to a more secure and empowered outlook on life.

- **Make a change:** Liberated from outdated societal norms that once held you back, you may experience a profound sense of freedom, allowing you to embrace change and take on the world with confidence. No longer confined by the expectations of the past, you may be empowered to chart your own course towards financial success and independence.

Are you ready? Let's take the first step together!

CHAPTER 2

Financial foundations

As you navigate the intricate landscape of mortgages, doubts and uncertainties may naturally surface, yet hidden within these challenges lies the potential for profound growth and empowerment.

Reflecting on my own journey, I grappled with financial uncertainties and lacked the confidence to navigate the complexities of personal finance. Like many people, I

Unfortunately, it took me a long
time to realise the importance
of taking proactive steps to
improve my financial situation,
during which countless
opportunities for growth
slipped through my fingers.

---

yearned for a clear and actionable game plan to guide me towards financial security and prosperity.

Unfortunately, it took me a long time to realise the importance of taking proactive steps to improve my financial situation, during which countless opportunities for growth slipped through my fingers.

It's this realisation that fuels my passion to equip you with a game plan born from firsthand experience.

I call this: 'Financial Foundations: Crafting a Game plan for Growing Financial Confidence'. It is Stage Two in a signature system I have developed called 'The Brava Finance Way'. It's a process I walk my customers through that strives to help them assume control of their finances as part of their journey (back) into the property market.

In my experience, I believe this stage is crucial for setting the groundwork for your financial journey. It involves a comprehensive evaluation of your current financial situation, establishing a clear vision for your financial future, and building robust financial habits. By creating a strong financial foundation, you can move forward with informed decisions and strategic actions that align with your long-term goals more confidently.

Join me as we embark on a journey to craft solid financial foundations and cultivate unwavering confidence in managing your finances.

Please note I am not a financial adviser. The aim of my game plan is to help you take that first step, to change your mindset and start the action that I believe is required for improving your financial confidence. Following these steps in my game plan does not mean you will automatically achieve financial security. It is intended to be a guide only.

These are the steps I took to improve my financial confidence and security.

Step 1: Assess your starting point

Creating a baseline is the very first step you should take. You will need to:

Reflect on your current financial situation

- Take the time to sit down and reflect on where you currently stand financially. This includes understanding your overall financial health, your financial goals, and any concerns or challenges you may be facing.

- Consider factors such as your sources of income, your spending habits, your saving and investing behaviours, as well as any debts or financial obligations you may have.

Evaluate your income, expenses, assets and liabilities

- Income: Calculate your total monthly income from all sources, including wages, bonuses, investments, rental income, etc.

- Expenses: Track your monthly expenses across various categories, such as housing, utilities, transportation, groceries, entertainment, debt repayments, etc. This helps in understanding where your money is going and where you might be able to make adjustments.

- Assets: List all your assets, including cash savings, investments, retirement accounts, real estate properties, vehicles, valuable possessions, etc.

- Liabilities: Make a list of all your liabilities or debts, such as mortgages, car loans, credit card debt, student loans, personal loans, etc. Include the outstanding balance, interest rates, and monthly payments for each.

Identify your strengths and weaknesses

- Take stock of your financial habits and behaviours. Identify areas where you are doing well and areas where you could improve.

- Consider your strengths, such as consistent saving habits, strong budgeting skills, or a good understanding of investment principles.

Identify any specific areas where you feel less confident or knowledgeable. This could include topics like investing in the stock market, understanding different types of insurance policies, or planning for retirement.

- Also, recognise your weaknesses, such as overspending tendencies, a lack of emergency savings, or avoidance of financial planning.

Assess your financial skills and knowledge gaps

- Evaluate your level of financial literacy and your understanding of key financial concepts, such as budgeting, investing, debt management, insurance, taxes, retirement planning, etc.

- Identify any specific areas where you feel less confident or knowledgeable. This could include topics like investing in the stock market, understanding different types of insurance policies, or planning for retirement.

- Consider seeking out resources, courses or professional advice to fill these knowledge gaps and improve your financial literacy.

Step 2: Create a vision

You can create a vision for your financial future by setting financial goals. This requires you to:

Visualise the life you want

- Take some time to visualise your ideal life. What does financial security look like to you? This could include aspects such as owning a home, travelling the world, starting a business, supporting your family, retiring comfortably, or having the freedom to pursue your passions without financial constraints.

- Consider not only material possessions but also experiences, relationships and personal fulfilment that contribute to your overall sense of well-being and happiness.

Clearly define your financial goals

- Once you have a clear vision of your desired lifestyle and financial security, translate these aspirations into specific, measurable financial goals. These goals should be realistic, achievable, and aligned with your values and priorities.

- Break down your goals into short-term, medium-term and long-term objectives. Short-term goals may include building an emergency fund or paying off high-interest debt, while long-term goals could involve saving for retirement or purchasing a home.

- Visualise yourself achieving these goals and imagine how your life will be transformed as a result. This can help you to stay focused on, and committed to, your financial plan.

Embrace a modern mindset

- Challenge any outdated beliefs or misconceptions you may have about money and finance. Recognise that financial success is attainable regardless of your background, gender or past financial mistakes.

- Embrace a growth mindset that emphasises learning, adaptability and resilience. Understand that financial planning is a dynamic process that requires continuous education, self-reflection and adjustment.

- Seek inspiration and guidance from modern financial role models, thought leaders and resources that promote inclusivity, diversity and empowerment in personal finance.

Be realistic and flexible with
your budget, allowing room
for unexpected expenses
or changes in income.

Step 3: Build a foundation

You can build a solid foundation by establishing healthy financial habits. Below are some tips that I found useful in my own journey, which I'll share with you in a general sense:

Budgeting

- Start by tracking your income and expenses to understand your current spending patterns. This doesn't need to be fancy – a simple spreadsheet does the job!

- Create a budget that outlines your income sources and allocates funds for essential expenses, savings, debt repayment and discretionary spending.

- Be realistic and flexible with your budget, allowing room for unexpected expenses or changes in income.

- Regularly review your budget and adjust as needed to ensure it continues to reflect your financial goals and priorities.

Saving and investing

- Set savings goals for both short-term needs (emergency fund, holiday, etc.) and long-term objectives (retirement, children's education, etc.).

- If you're able to comfortably put aside savings, creating an automated transfer may help your savings be more consistent.

- If you're in the position to dabble into investing, or wanting to learn more about what your goals or risk tolerance are, visiting the link below can show you what popular investment choices Australians are making and why. https://www.forbes.com/advisor/au/investing/best-low-risk-investments-for-australians/

- Monitoring your investments is very important for staying on top of your finances. It's recommended to receive professional financial advice before making adjustments to your strategy to stay on track with your financial objectives.

Explore strategies such as the debt snowball method (paying off the smallest debts first) or the debt avalanche method (paying off the debts with the highest interest rates first) that may accelerate debt repayment.

Debt management

- Take inventory of your existing debts, including balances, interest rates and minimum monthly payments.

- Prioritise debt repayment based on factors such as interest rates, loan terms and financial goals.

- Consider debt consolidation options to streamline multiple debts into a single, more manageable payment with a lower interest rate.

- Explore strategies such as the debt snowball method (paying off the smallest debts first) or the debt avalanche method (paying off the debts with the highest interest rates first) that may accelerate debt repayment.

- Avoid taking on new debt whenever possible and focus on living within your means to prevent further financial strain.

Step 4: Educate yourself

Investing in financial literacy and self-development is an essential step in boosting your financial confidence. You can:

Pursue learning opportunities

- Take advantage of a wide range of resources available for financial education, including books, online courses, webinars, workshops, podcasts and educational websites.

- Look for reputable sources of information that provide comprehensive coverage of personal finance topics, such as budgeting, saving, investing, retirement planning and tax management.

- Consider starting with foundational books or courses that cover basic financial concepts before diving into more advanced topics.

- Explore specialised resources tailored to your specific interests or needs, such as investing in real estate, starting a business or managing debt.

Consider working with a financial adviser or planner who can provide personalised guidance and advice based on your individual financial situation, goals and risk tolerance.

Seek personalised guidance and support

- Consider working with a financial adviser or planner who can provide personalised guidance and advice based on your individual financial situation, goals and risk tolerance.

- A professional adviser can help you develop a customised financial plan, implement investment strategies, navigate complex financial decisions, and adapt to changes in your circumstances over time.

- Seek recommendations from trusted sources or professional associations, and conduct thorough research to find an adviser with the right qualifications, experience and approach to meet your needs.

Stay informed

- Stay informed about current events, economic trends and market developments that may impact your financial decisions and investments.

- Follow reputable financial news outlets, subscribe to newsletters, and utilise financial apps or platforms that provide real-time updates and analysis.

- Join online communities, forums or social media groups dedicated to personal finance and investment discussions to stay connected with peers and experts in the field.

- Attend industry conferences, seminars or networking events to gain insights, exchange ideas, and stay abreast of emerging opportunities and best practices.

Step 5: Take action

You can implement your personalised financial plan in the following ways:

Set priorities

- Review your financial goals and prioritise them based on urgency, importance and feasibility.

- Break down each goal into smaller, manageable tasks or action steps.

- Develop a timeline for achieving each goal and allocate resources accordingly, such as time, money and effort.

- Focus on taking consistent and disciplined actions to make progress towards your goals, even if they are small steps forward.

- Regularly reassess your priorities and adjust your plan as needed to stay aligned with your evolving circumstances and aspirations.

Address obstacles

- Anticipate potential challenges or obstacles that may arise on your financial journey, such as unexpected

Celebrating milestones can
help boost your motivation,
reinforce positive behaviours,
and build momentum
towards future success.

expenses, market fluctuations, or changes in personal circumstances.

- Develop strategies to overcome these challenges, such as building an emergency fund, diversifying your investments, or seeking additional sources of income.

- Be flexible and adaptable in your approach, willing to adjust your plan or pivot if circumstances change or if certain strategies are not yielding the desired results.

- Seek support from trusted advisers, mentors or peers to brainstorm solutions and provide encouragement during difficult times.

Celebrate milestones

- Take time to acknowledge and celebrate each milestone and achievement along your financial journey, no matter how small.

- Celebrating milestones can help boost your motivation, reinforce positive behaviours, and build momentum towards future success.

- Find meaningful ways to reward yourself for reaching milestones, whether it's treating yourself to a small indulgence, taking a break to relax and recharge, or sharing your achievements with loved ones.

- Reflect on how far you've come and use each milestone as an opportunity to reaffirm your commitment to your financial goals and aspirations.

Surrounding yourself with positive and empowering content can help reshape your mindset and inspire you to pursue your own financial goals.

Step 6: Connect with others

The journey to financial confidence and security doesn't have to be a lonely one. On the contrary, you should:

Curate your social media feed

- Take control of your social media experience by curating your feed to include accounts of inspirational women who have achieved financial independence.

- Follow successful female entrepreneurs, investors and financial experts who share their journeys, insights and strategies for building wealth.

- Surrounding yourself with positive and empowering content can help reshape your mindset and inspire you to pursue your own financial goals.

Seek mentorship and guidance

- Look for opportunities to connect with inspirational women in your community or online who have achieved financial success.

- Engage with them through networking events, webinars or mentorship programs to learn from their experiences and gain valuable insights into navigating the path towards financial independence.

- Having role models and mentors can provide encouragement, guidance and support as you work towards your goals.

Take inspired action

- Use the inspiration and knowledge gained from engaging with inspirational women to take action towards your own financial independence.

- Set specific, achievable goals based on the examples and advice shared by these women. Break down your goals into actionable steps and consistently work towards them.

- Maintain your motivation by staying connected with the supportive community of women who are also on their journey towards financial empowerment.

Step 7: Maintain your focus

If you're truly determined to rewrite your financial narrative, you must:

Continuously evaluate your progress

- Regularly review your financial goals, objectives and the action steps outlined in your financial plan to assess your progress.

- Track your financial metrics, such as savings rate, investment returns, debt reduction and net worth, to gauge how effectively you're moving towards your goals.

- Identify areas where you're excelling and areas where you may be falling short of your targets.

- Reflect on any changes in your circumstances or priorities that may require adjustments to your financial plan.

Adjust your strategy as needed

- Be open to modifying your financial plan in response to changes in your circumstances, financial markets or external factors.

- If you encounter obstacles or challenges, reassess your approach and consider alternative strategies to overcome them.

- Stay flexible and adaptable in your thinking, willing to pivot or make course corrections as necessary to stay on track with your goals.

- Seek advice from financial professionals or mentors to help you navigate complex decisions and make informed adjustments to your strategy.

Stay proactive in pursuing financial success

- Take ownership of your financial well-being by actively engaging with your finances and taking proactive steps to improve your financial situation.

- Keep yourself informed about changes in tax laws, investment opportunities, and other relevant financial developments that may impact your strategy.

Challenging outdated mindsets
can make a big difference to
building financial confidence.
Taking action, continuously
evaluating progress,
and remaining proactive
throughout the process ensure
adaptability and resilience
in the face of challenges.

- Continuously seek opportunities for growth and improvement, whether through further education, skill development, or exploring new avenues for income generation or wealth accumulation.

- Cultivate a mindset of resilience and determination, recognising that financial success often requires persistence, patience, and the ability to adapt to changing circumstances.

> Through the establishment of healthy financial habits and ongoing investment in financial literacy, you can lay a solid foundation for long-term success.

By following this framework, you can build greater financial confidence and empowerment. Starting with a thorough assessment of your current financial situation, followed by setting clear goals, you can create a roadmap tailored to your aspirations. Through the establishment of healthy financial habits and ongoing investment in financial literacy, you can lay a solid foundation for long-term success. Challenging outdated mindsets can make a big difference to building financial confidence. Taking action, continuously evaluating progress, and remaining proactive throughout the process ensure adaptability and resilience in the face of challenges. Ultimately, by committing to this holistic approach, you are working towards unlocking your full financial potential, achieving more stability and, ultimately, more fulfilment in your life.

Remember, the ultimate prize is financial confidence and security! In creating a solid game plan, you are more likely to embrace a modern money mindset and make more-informed decisions, putting you a step closer to achieving financial freedom.

In the next chapter, we start to look at the wonderful world of mortgages in more detail, with a comprehensive list of mortgage-related terms and phrases. I also highlight some of the key benefits of working with a mortgage broker ... would be rude not to lol!

CHAPTER 3

Demystifying the world of mortgages

The world of mortgages is unfamiliar territory for many people, and has enough jargon to fill volumes. The technical language can be overwhelming, but fear not! Understanding mortgage jargon is not only achievable, but essential for making informed decisions about one of life's most significant financial commitments ... buying a home.

In the first half of this chapter, I share a comprehensive list of the most commonly used mortgage terms and their definitions, serving as your reliable guide to navigate these complexities with more confidence and clarity. Then, in the second half of the chapter, I highlight some of the advantages of engaging a mortgage broker.

Glossary of terms

Let's dive in and explore the language of mortgages together, ensuring you're well-equipped to navigate your path towards home ownership...

Mortgage: A legal agreement by which a bank/lender/ creditor lends money at interest in exchange for taking the title of the debtor's property.

Principal: The initial amount of money borrowed, excluding interest. Your mortgage principal is the amount you borrow from a lender to buy your home. If a bank lends you $250,000, your mortgage principal is $250,000. You'll pay this amount off in monthly instalments for a predetermined length of time (loan term).

Principal and interest (P&I) loan: A home loan consists of two components: principal and interest. Principal is the loan amount you have borrowed from the bank or lender, and interest is the cost charged by the bank for borrowing that principal.

Interest-only (IO) loan: A mortgage repayment option where only the interest (and not the principal) is paid for a specified period.

Interest rate: The percentage of the loan amount charged by the lender for the use of their money.

Loan term: The period over which a loan is to be repaid, typically expressed in years. The most common loan period is 30 years.

Loan repayment: The monthly instalment paid by the borrower to the lender to repay the loan.

Owner-occupied (OO) home loan: A type of loan associated with a property intended as a personal residence.

Investment (INV) loan: A type of loan linked to a property intended for purposes other than as a personal residence.

Loan-to-value ratio (LVR): The ratio of the loan amount to the appraised value of the property. E.g. if your loan amount is $500,000 and your property value is $1,000,000, then your LVR is 50%.

Fixed-rate mortgage: A mortgage with an interest rate that is fixed or stable for the entire term of the loan. Typically it is for a period of one to five years.

Variable-rate mortgage: A mortgage with an interest rate that can change periodically.

Split loan: A mortgage that is divided into two or more portions, each with different interest rates or loan types. For example, a percentage of the loan on a fixed rate and a percentage of the loan on a variable rate.

Comparison rate: An interest rate figure that includes both the interest rate and most fees and charges relating to a loan.

Revert rate: The variable rate your loan reverts to once the fixed-rate period has expired.

Lenders mortgage insurance (LMI): Insurance paid by the borrower that protects the lender in case the borrower defaults on the loan, typically required for loans with a high loan-to-value ratio (LVR) – above 80%.

Equity: The difference between the market value of a property and the amount owed on the mortgage.

Offset account: A savings or transaction account linked to a mortgage, where the balance offsets the interest payable on the loan, which reduces the amount of interest you pay over the life of the loan.

Redraw facility: A feature of a loan account that allows borrowers to withdraw extra payments made on their mortgage. Works similarly to an offset account where the balance offsets the interest payable on the loan, which reduces the amount of interest you pay over the life of the loan.

Stamp duty: A state government tax on property transactions. This varies between states.

Conveyancing: The legal process of transferring property ownership from seller to buyer.

Mortgage broker: A financial intermediary (in other words, a 'go between') who works with customers to find a mortgage solution with their best interests at heart. A mortgage broker must operate under BID (see the next definition).

Best interest duty (BID): A statutory obligation for mortgage brokers to act in the best interests of consumers (best interests duty), and to prioritise consumers' interests when providing credit assistance (conflict priority rule).

Break costs: Charges incurred when a borrower pays off a fixed-rate mortgage before the end of the agreed term.

Exit fees: Charges incurred when a borrower pays off a mortgage, particularly if it is paid off before a specified period.

Default: Failure to meet the terms of a loan agreement, often resulting in penalties.

Title deed: A legal document proving ownership of a property.

Home loan application/settlement fee: A fee charged by the lender to cover the cost of processing a mortgage application.

Australian Government Home Guarantee Scheme (HGS): An Australian Government initiative to support eligible home buyers to buy a home sooner. The scheme includes three types of guarantees:

- First Home Guarantee (FHG) – supporting eligible first home buyers to buy a home sooner.

- Regional First Home Buyer Guarantee (RFHBG) – supporting eligible regional first home buyers to buy a home sooner, in a regional area.

- Family Home Guarantee (FHG) – supporting eligible single parents or eligible single legal guardians of at least one dependent to buy a home sooner.

Bridging loan: A short-term loan that helps borrowers finance the purchase of a new property while waiting to sell their existing one.

Construction loan: A type of loan that provides funds for the construction of a new property or significant renovations.

Deposit: The upfront amount paid by a borrower towards the purchase price of a property.

Servicing guarantor: A person who agrees to take responsibility for the mortgage repayments if the borrower defaults.

Security guarantor: A family member with sufficient equity in their home can use it as a security guarantee for the borrower's loan.

Home loan package: A bundled offer that includes a mortgage loan along with additional banking products and services.

Mortgagee: The lender or financial institution that provides the mortgage loan.

Mortgagor: The borrower who pledges their property as security for the mortgage loan.

Refinance: The process of switching from one mortgage lender to another or changing the terms of an existing mortgage.

Valuation: The assessment of a property's value by a qualified valuer.

Aggregator: An aggregator acts as an intermediary between lenders and mortgage and finance brokers, and holds an Australian credit licence (ACL) with the Australian Securities and Investments Commission (ASIC). As an Australian credit licensee, an aggregator may appoint credit representatives (mortgage and finance brokers) who use their Australian credit licence to provide credit assistance.

Property settlement: Completion of the purchase of a property, when it officially becomes yours.

Conditional approval/pre-approval: This means that your mortgage underwriter is mostly satisfied with your mortgage application. They are willing to approve your mortgage as long as you can meet their pending conditions.

Unconditional/formal approval: The lender's final decision to approve you for the loan. It means they have taken all your details into account and are happy to lend you a set amount of money to buy a specific property.

Debt consolidation: A mortgage refinancing option where you consolidate all your existing debts into one loan.

Cash-out refinance: A mortgage refinancing option that lets you convert home equity into cash.

As you familiarise yourself with the essential mortgage terms outlined here, you're taking a significant step towards building financial confidence. Remember, knowledge is power. By understanding the language of mortgages, you're better equipped to make informed decisions that align with your financial goals and aspirations.

The road ahead may have its twists and turns, but, armed with the right knowledge, you're well-prepared to navigate it with confidence.

> Building a strong foundation of mortgage literacy sets the stage for a confident and empowered journey into home ownership.

But don't stop here. Continue to engage with the material, ask questions, and seek guidance when needed. Building a strong foundation of mortgage literacy sets the stage for a confident and empowered journey into home ownership. So, pat yourself on the back for the progress you've made, and stay committed to your financial journey. The road ahead may have its twists and turns, but, armed with the right knowledge, you're well-prepared to navigate it with confidence.

Your financial ally (aka your wingwoman)

I liken the role of a mortgage broker, or financial ally, to that of a wingman or wingwoman – let's combine this: wing(wo)man. The concept of a wing(wo)man may not be officially recognised in the dictionary, but its essence resonates deeply in both aviation and everyday life. Traditionally, a wingman in aviation serves as a form of protective support, flying just outside and behind the right wing of the leading aircraft in a flight formation. In slang terminology, a wingman is someone who helps, protects or guides a friend or associate through various situations.

In the context of mortgage brokers, the role remains the same: to offer invaluable support and guidance, especially in significant endeavours such as buying a property … or refinancing. Purchasing a home isn't a decision made overnight; it's a process that involves careful planning and consideration.

This process can be daunting, and is influenced by factors such as individual experience, knowledge, confidence levels and financial situation. For some, the idea of buying a house may remain just that – an idea – due to uncertainty or lack of direction. Yet, it's precisely in these moments that having a wing(wo)man by your side can make all the difference.

Think of your wing(wo)man as your adviser, your confidant, your partner in navigating the complexities of financing a property. From the outset, they can assist you in formulating a game plan, providing clarity on the steps involved, and bolstering your confidence every step of the way.

3 key roles of your mortgage broker

The right mortgage broker can completely transform the way you navigate the world of mortgages. Think of your mortgage broker as your:

Personal home loan shopper

Mortgage brokers have access to many different lenders, so we can do the legwork for you. In addition to understanding different lender policies and niches, our established relationships with lenders allow us to potentially negotiate more favourable terms on your behalf.

A mortgage broker is like having a personal stylist by your side. They understand your style preferences, budget and so on, and tailor your shopping experience accordingly.

As outlined in the previous section, we must operate under best interest duty (BID) to ensure our recommendations are within your best interests – something a lender does not need to abide by. It is also an opportunity to find a lender with products that fit your needs – rather than being forced to fit within the product policy of one particular lender that you have liaised directly with. That's like going to a shopping centre to buy an outfit for a special occasion but only going to one shop! In contrast, a mortgage broker is like having a personal stylist by your side. They understand your style preferences, budget and so on, and tailor your shopping experience accordingly. In other words, they create a personalised solution that's right for you.

Professional admin assistant

A mortgage broker will manage the collection of information from you, organise it all, go through the relevant checks and balances to ensure a strong application, prepare and submit the loan application on your behalf, and follow the application right through to settlement. Job done!

Ongoing loan adviser

Your relationship with a mortgage broker doesn't end once settlement occurs. A mortgage broker can act as a loan adviser for the life of your loan, providing ongoing support and guidance. They can periodically review your loan to ensure it remains competitive, and present refinance options if it is not.

And the best part is that the lender will pay the mortgage broker's commission – you don't need to pay for this service!

An essential checklist

Taking on a mortgage is a huge commitment, so it's important that you trust your mortgage broker. Before you choose one to work with, I recommend you check the following:

- Their credit representative number. Once you have this number, you can look them up on the ASIC website (www.asic.gov.au) to confirm they are who they say they are. My credit representative number is 540557.

- Their qualifications. Ask for a copy of their Certificate IV in Mortgage Broking and Finance, which is the minimum requirement they must have. As an FYI, I also have my Diploma of Finance and Mortgage Broking Management.

- Ensure they're registered with an ASIC-approved dispute resolution scheme, such as the Australian Financial Complaints Authority (AFCA). I belong to AFCA and my membership number is 104841.

- Ensure they are registered with an ASIC-approved industry association, such as the Mortgage & Finance Association of Australia (MFAA) or the Finance Brokers Association of Australia (FBAA). I belong to the MFAA and my membership number is 602414.

In my experience as a mortgage broker, I often find myself working closely with my customers long before they embark on the journey of purchasing a home. I take them through my signature process of building financial confidence, which I outlined in the previous chapter. I prioritise education, helping my customers gain a deeper understanding of their financial situation and goals to ultimately boost their financial confidence. Together, we develop a tailored plan to bridge the gap between their current circumstances and their desired outcome, all

Buying a property is one of life's significant milestones, and you don't have to go it alone. Having a wing(wo)man by your side can transform what might feel like a solitary journey into a collaborative and empowering experience.

while challenging outdated notions about finances that may be holding them back.

Buying a property is one of life's significant milestones, and you don't have to go it alone. Having a wing(wo)man by your side can transform what might feel like a solitary journey into a collaborative and empowering experience. It's a reminder that seeking support is not a sign of weakness, but a demonstration of strength – a recognition that together, we can achieve more than we ever could alone.

> So, if you find yourself hesitating to take that first step towards home ownership, remember that you don't have to navigate this path solo.

So, if you find yourself hesitating to take that first step towards home ownership, remember that you don't have to navigate this path solo. Reach out, find your wing(wo)man, and embark on this journey with confidence, knowing that you have an ally by your side every step of the way.

In the next chapter, I reveal the steps involved in purchasing a property, as well as the steps required to refinance an existing mortgage.

CHAPTER 4

A guide to purchasing and refinancing

Embarking on the journey of purchasing a property can be both exhilarating and daunting. From arranging finances to celebrating the moment you receive the keys to your new home, each step is pivotal in realising your dream of home ownership.

In the first section of this chapter, we'll delve into the sequential process of acquiring property and explore the steps involved. Then, in the second section, we'll look at the steps required to refinance. In the final section, I reveal the 'Brava Finance Way' – a four-step process I use to help my customers successfully purchase a property or refinance their existing mortgage.

Let's get to it!

Key steps to purchasing a property

Navigating the steps of a property purchase can be a transformative journey, paving the way for a future filled with security and possibility. By familiarising yourself with these essential steps and seeking professional guidance along the way, you can navigate the complexities of property transactions with more confidence and clarity. Remember, each milestone brings you closer to the realisation of your home ownership dreams, marking the beginning of a new chapter filled with endless opportunities and cherished memories.

Arrange finances

Before diving into the property search, it's crucial to assess your financial readiness. Consulting with a mortgage broker may streamline this process, providing insights into your borrowing capacity and securing pre-approval for a home loan. This not only sets a realistic budget for your property search but also demonstrates your commitment to sellers, bolstering your confidence as you embark on this journey. Additionally, don't forget to

Navigating the legal intricacies
of property transactions requires
expert guidance. Engage
a solicitor or conveyancer
early on to oversee the legal
aspects of the purchase.

factor in additional costs, such as stamp duty, legal fees and inspections, to avoid any surprises along the way.

Engage professionals

Navigating the legal intricacies of property transactions requires expert guidance. Engage a solicitor or conveyancer early on to oversee the legal aspects of the purchase. Similarly, enlisting the expertise of a real estate agent or buyer's agent can potentially streamline your property search, ensuring you find the right match for your needs and preferences.

Undergo research and planning

Armed with your budget and professional support, it's time to delve into research and planning. Explore the property market, both online and offline, to gain insights into prevailing trends and pricing. Define your criteria, including location preferences and property features, to narrow down your options effectively. Attend open houses and inspections to gauge the market firsthand and refine your search criteria accordingly.

Make an offer

Once you've identified a property that meets your criteria, it's time to make your move. Whether through a written offer or bidding at auction, initiate negotiations with the seller to secure the property. Work closely with your real estate agent or solicitor/conveyancer to navigate the negotiation process and reach a mutually beneficial agreement.

Complete the contract of sale

With negotiations concluded, the seller's solicitor or conveyancer will prepare a contract of sale. Review this document meticulously with your legal representative and address any concerns or discrepancies. Upon mutual agreement, both parties sign the contract, and you'll typically pay a deposit, solidifying your commitment to the purchase.

Conduct property inspections

Prior to finalising the purchase, arrange for building and pest inspections to assess the property's condition thoroughly. These inspections serve as safeguards against potential issues and provide peace of mind as you progress towards settlement.

Finalise finance

With the contract of sale in place, it's time to progress from pre-approval to formal/unconditional approval with your lender. Provide all necessary documentation and liaise closely with your mortgage broker to help navigate this stage. Securing unconditional approval solidifies your financial readiness for settlement.

Utilise the cooling-off period (if applicable)

Depending on your location, you may have a cooling-off period following the exchange of contracts. Utilise this window to conduct further due diligence or seek legal advice if needed. Keep in mind that withdrawing from the contract during this period may incur penalties.

Finalise legal aspects

As settlement approaches, your solicitor or conveyancer will conduct final checks on the property title and ensure all legal requirements are met. They'll facilitate the necessary documentation and oversee the settlement process on your behalf.

Complete settlement

On the designated settlement day, the remaining balance of the purchase price is paid, and legal ownership of the property is transferred to you. This milestone marks the culmination of your property purchase journey and heralds the beginning of your new chapter as a homeowner.

Officially take possession

With settlement completed, you'll receive the keys to your new home and officially take possession of the property. This momentous occasion symbolises the realisation of your home ownership aspirations and sets the stage for creating cherished memories in your new abode.

Celebrate and move in

Amid the whirlwind of emotions, take a moment to celebrate this significant milestone. Whether with family, friends or a quiet toast to yourself, acknowledge the achievement of home ownership and embrace the excitement of moving into your new home.

Notify authorities

As you settle into your new abode, don't forget to notify the relevant authorities of your change of address. Update utility providers, local councils and any other pertinent entities to ensure a seamless transition to your new residence.

Amid the whirlwind of emotions, take a moment to celebrate this significant milestone.

Key steps to refinancing your mortgage

Given your mortgage is most likely your largest financial commitment, it is important to ensure its health is in tip-top shape and you're not paying the bank more than you need to! I have developed a 'Mortgage Health Assessment' quiz to check your mortgage health against five key areas. You can complete the short quiz here: https://cara-dib0lezt.scoreapp.com

Refinancing your mortgage can be a strategic move to potentially improve your financial situation and secure a loan more aligned with your best interests. Whether you're enticed by competitive rates from other lenders or seeking to adapt to changes in your circumstances, the steps outlined here can guide you through this process.

So, why consider refinancing? Perhaps you've noticed tantalising new customer rates advertised by other banks, sparking your interest in exploring more competitive options. Alternatively, changes in your financial landscape may prompt you to seek out loan products more tailored to your current needs. Whatever your motivation, taking

By navigating the steps of
a refinance with diligence
and foresight, you can
unlock newfound financial
freedom which may position
you for a brighter future.

the first step towards a refinance is pivotal. You can choose to walk through this process on your own, directly with a lender, or alongside a mortgage broker who can help widen your search and guide you along the way – essentially doing the leg work for you. By navigating the steps of a refinance with diligence and foresight, you can unlock newfound financial freedom which may position you for a brighter future.

Assess your current loan

The journey begins with a thorough assessment of your current loan. Reviewing its product features and benefits, terms, interest rate and associated fees lays the groundwork for understanding your refinancing potential. It's a good time to contact your current lender to try to negotiate more favourable terms.

Set clear goals

This should be followed by clearly determining your goals – do you want to reduce monthly payments to improve your cashflow, access equity, change your loan product to better suit your interests, or secure a more competitive rate?

Check your credit score

Checking your credit score is the next crucial step. A healthy credit score may enhance your refinancing prospects, while addressing any issues can help boost your financial standing.

Conduct market research

Armed with this information, the next step is to conduct market research, exploring interest rates and loan products offered by various lenders. Consider features that align with your goals, weighing potential savings against associated costs.

> Consider features that align with your goals, weighing potential savings against associated costs.

Understand the implications

Understanding the financial implications of refinancing is super important. Be clear on costs like mortgage discharge fees, application fees and valuation charges, weighing them up with potential savings over the loan's lifespan. Additionally, ensure your financial situation aligns with

---

Choosing the right
lender is pivotal to your
refinancing success.

---

the lender's criteria, satisfying stress tests to demonstrate serviceability.

Get your property valued

Property valuation is a critical stage, and determines your property's current market value and loan-to-value ratio (LVR). A lower LVR is typically viewed by the lender as less risk and could potentially result in more favourable loan terms. Your mortgage broker can help you with this.

Choose the right lender

Choosing the right lender is pivotal to your refinancing success. Carefully evaluate their terms and conditions, policy niche and products, and consider both traditional banks and non-bank lenders.

Secure conditional approval

Once you've made your selection, submit your application, providing comprehensive documentation to support your case. The first step after the application has been submitted is conditional approval. Conditional approval means that a lender has agreed, in principle, to lend you money but hasn't proceeded to full or final approval.

There are typically conditions that need to be met before moving to formal (unconditional) approval.

Secure unconditional approval

Formal (unconditional) approval means that the lender has formally assessed your paperwork and signed off on your loan application. In short, they have decided to proceed with your home loan after conditions have been met and are happy with their assessment. It is at this stage that you receive a loan offer and contract for signing. You can then set up new bank accounts as directed by your lender, preparing for the settlement of the new loan.

Stay proactive

As the refinancing process unfolds, stay proactive in monitoring progress and addressing any queries promptly.

Settle the new loan and celebrate

Settlement day is the day your new home loan is used to pay off your existing home loan. Typically, your new lender will do all the leg work for you. This includes: liaising with your previous lender to pay out and discharge your previous home loan as well as registering a new mortgage for your property. Make sure you celebrate the successful refinancing endeavour, embracing the potential benefits it brings. Remember to update any automatic payments or direct debits associated with your old loan, helping to ensure a seamless transition to your new financial arrangement.

> Make sure you celebrate the successful refinancing endeavour, embracing the potential benefits it brings.

The 'Brava Finance Way':
My 4-step signature process

BF

BRAVA FINANCE

The ' Brava Finance Way'

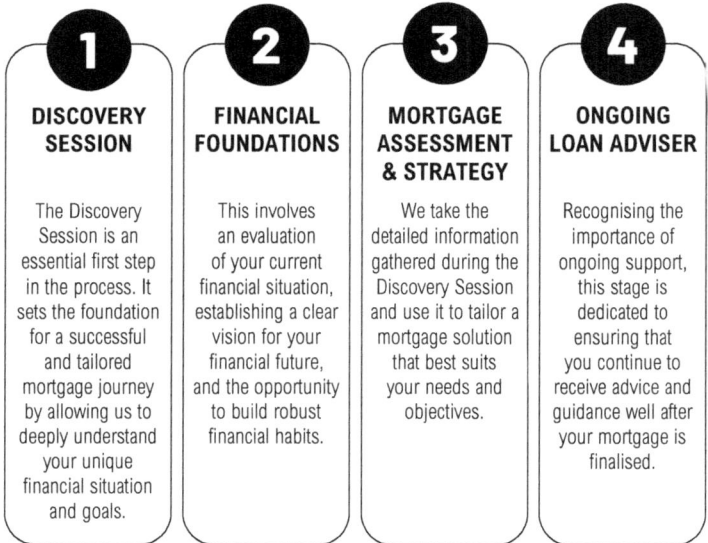

1	**2**	**3**	**4**
DISCOVERY SESSION	**FINANCIAL FOUNDATIONS**	**MORTGAGE ASSESSMENT & STRATEGY**	**ONGOING LOAN ADVISER**
The Discovery Session is an essential first step in the process. It sets the foundation for a successful and tailored mortgage journey by allowing us to deeply understand your unique financial situation and goals.	This involves an evaluation of your current financial situation, establishing a clear vision for your financial future, and the opportunity to build robust financial habits.	We take the detailed information gathered during the Discovery Session and use it to tailor a mortgage solution that best suits your needs and objectives.	Recognising the importance of ongoing support, this stage is dedicated to ensuring that you continue to receive advice and guidance well after your mortgage is finalised.

SUPPORT, ADVICE & EDUCATION

So, you are keen to buy a property or refinance your existing mortgage, but you've heard it's a long and exhausting process. And even though there are savings to be had with a new lender, you aren't sure you have the time and energy required to refinance.

Yes, I hear this many times a day... It's a common objection!

As a result, I wanted to flip this objection on its head by striving to develop a finely tuned, efficient and effective process from initial discussion to settlement – and beyond. At each stage of the process, I have mapped out customer touchpoints to ensure the right level of support, advice and education is delivered.

I call it 'The Brava Finance Way' (no prize for most innovative name here!). It was developed using a four-step methodology for the customer journey. Here I have outlined a summary of each of the stages to help you understand what is involved. I have already touched on key components of this during previous chapters, but I wanted to show you how it all comes together as part of my process. Let's dive into each stage:

Stage 1: Discovery Session

The Discovery Session is an essential first step in our mortgage service process. It sets the foundation for a successful and tailored mortgage journey by allowing

Our primary aim is to establish
a clear baseline from which
we can craft a personalised
plan that aligns with your
aspirations and needs.

us to deeply understand your unique financial situation and goals. This initial meeting is designed to be comprehensive and collaborative, ensuring that every aspect of your financial picture is considered. Our primary aim is to establish a clear baseline from which we can craft a personalised plan that aligns with your aspirations and needs.

Here are some of the key objectives of the Discovery Session.

Understanding your financial position and goals

During the Discovery Session, we will engage in a detailed discussion about your current financial position and your future goals. This includes exploring your financial aspirations, the level of support and education you require throughout the process, and any specific needs and objectives you have. By understanding what you hope to achieve, whether it's buying your first home, upgrading to a larger property, or investing in real estate, we can tailor our lending advice and strategies to best support your journey.

Comprehensive information gathering

A critical component of this session is gathering all relevant financial information. We will collect detailed data on your income, savings, employment history, existing debts and credit history. This comprehensive assessment allows us to get a clear picture of your financial health and borrowing capacity. It's important to be thorough at this stage, as the information we gather will directly influence the recommendations and strategies we develop for you.

Evaluating borrowing capacity

With all the necessary information in hand, we will then evaluate your current borrowing capacity. This involves analysing your financial data to determine how much you can realistically borrow, what kind of loan terms you might qualify for, and what your repayment capabilities are. This assessment is crucial for setting realistic expectations and ensuring that you are well-prepared for the financial commitment of purchasing a property.

Developing a strategic plan

Finally, based on the insights gained during the Discovery Session, we will develop a strategic plan tailored to your

The strategic plan serves as
a roadmap for your mortgage
journey, providing clear guidance
and actionable steps to help
you move forward confidently.

needs. This plan will outline the steps necessary to achieve your property purchase goals, including identifying the most suitable mortgage solutions. We will consider various loan products, interest rates and lenders to find the best fit for your situation. The strategic plan serves as a roadmap for your mortgage journey, providing clear guidance and actionable steps to help you move forward confidently.

By the end of the Discovery Session, you will have a solid understanding of your financial standing, a realistic view of your borrowing capacity and maximum purchase price, and a strategic plan tailored to your property purchase goals. This comprehensive approach ensures that we lay a strong foundation for your mortgage journey, setting you up for success from the very beginning.

> This comprehensive approach ensures that we lay a strong foundation for your mortgage journey, setting you up for success from the very beginning.

Stage 2: Financial Foundations

This has been covered already in Chapter 2, so I won't go into all the detail here, but it is an option if you would like a game plan (born from firsthand experience) to help improve financial confidence and get you ready for the next step!

A reminder of the program steps:

Assess your starting point

Evaluate your current financial situation to determine where you stand.

Create a vision

Define your financial goals and the future you want to achieve.

Build a foundation

Establish a solid financial base by managing debt and creating a budget.

Our primary aim is to ensure that you secure a mortgage lender and product that align with your best interests, while we manage the entire process on your behalf, from research to settlement.

Educate yourself

Gain knowledge about financial principles and strategies to make informed decisions.

Take action

Implement your financial plan with concrete steps and consistent effort.

Connect with others

Seek support and advice from financial professionals and like-minded individuals.

Maintain your focus

Regularly review and adjust your plan to stay on track towards your financial goals.

Stage 3: Mortgage Assessment and Strategy

This stage is where we take the detailed information gathered during the Discovery Session and use it to tailor a mortgage solution that best fits your needs and objectives. It is a crucial stage as it involves a thorough analysis of your financial situation and goals, allowing us to identify the most suitable mortgage options for you. Our primary aim is to ensure that you secure a mortgage lender and product that align with your best interests, while we manage the entire process on your behalf, from research to settlement.

Here are the key steps of the strategy.

Determining needs and objectives

Using the insights from the Discovery Session, we begin by clearly defining your specific needs and objectives. This involves a deep dive into your financial aspirations, your ideal loan term, and any particular features you desire in a mortgage product. We also consider your long-term financial goals and how the mortgage or refinance fits into your overall financial plan. By having a clear understanding of what you want to achieve, we can focus our efforts on finding a mortgage solution that is aligned with your needs.

Lender research

With your needs and objectives in mind, we conduct comprehensive research into potential lenders. This involves analysing a wide range of mortgage products from various banks, credit unions and non-bank lenders. We consider factors such as interest rates, loan terms, fees and flexibility of the mortgage products available. Additionally, as experienced mortgage brokers, we understand the unique policies and niches of different lenders, enabling us to match your specific situation with the most suitable lenders. This expertise is critical in ensuring that we present you with the most viable and beneficial options.

Lender options and recommendations

After thorough research, we compile a shortlist of the best lender options tailored to your needs. We will present these options to you, explaining the pros and cons of each lender and mortgage product. This includes detailed information on interest rates, repayment options, associated fees, and any special features or benefits. Leveraging our established relationships with lenders, we can also look to negotiate more favourable loan terms on your behalf. Based on this comprehensive analysis, we will recommend the most suitable options and work closely with you to choose the one that aligns best with your financial goals and circumstances.

Application management and settlement process

Once a lender and mortgage product have been selected, we take over the entire loan application and settlement process on your behalf. This includes preparing and submitting all necessary documentation, liaising with the lender, and ensuring that all requirements are met for a successful approval process. We manage every step, from application submission to loan approval and, ultimately, settlement. Our goal is to make this process as seamless and stress-free as possible, ensuring that you are well-prepared and confident as you move towards securing your property.

> Once a lender and mortgage product have been selected, we take over the entire loan application and settlement process on your behalf.

By the end of the Mortgage Assessment and Strategy stage, you will have a clear and actionable plan, a chosen lender, and a mortgage product that fits your needs. With our comprehensive management of the application and settlement process, coupled with our ability to potentially

Our goal is to foster a lasting relationship where you feel supported and informed throughout the life of your loan.

negotiate favourable terms, this allows you to focus on your property purchase with confidence.

Stage 4: Ongoing Loan Adviser

The journey of securing a mortgage doesn't end at settlement. In fact, it's just the beginning of a long-term financial commitment. Recognising the importance of ongoing support, this stage is dedicated to ensuring that you continue to receive advice and guidance well after your mortgage is finalised. This step underscores our commitment to building a lasting relationship with you, providing continual oversight and support to help you navigate the ever-changing financial landscape and keep your mortgage aligned with your evolving needs and goals.

Sustained support and relationship building

This stage represents the enduring commitment we have to our clients beyond the initial settlement of their mortgage. Unlike many brokers who view settlement as the conclusion of their service, we see it as just the beginning. Our goal is to foster a lasting relationship where you feel supported and informed throughout the life of your loan. This ongoing connection ensures that you always have a dedicated adviser to turn to with any questions or concerns about your mortgage or broader financial situation.

Regular loan reviews

An essential part of this stage is conducting periodic reviews of your mortgage. The financial landscape is dynamic, with interest rates and lending policies subject to frequent changes. By scheduling regular reviews, we can assess whether your current loan remains competitive and aligned with your financial goals. These reviews are an opportunity to evaluate your interest rate, loan features, and overall satisfaction with your lender. If more suitable options become available, we can guide you through the process of refinancing or renegotiating terms to ensure you continue to get the most suitable deal.

Personalised financial guidance

Beyond just managing your loan, we provide financial guidance for lending matters and strategic support for your broader financial well-being. This includes advice on how to leverage your home equity, as well as strategies that could pay down your mortgage more effectively. By understanding your overall financial picture, we can offer tailored advice that integrates your mortgage with your other financial goals.

Accessible and ongoing communication

Lastly, maintaining open lines of communication is crucial. We are always available to answer your questions, address concerns, and provide clarity on any aspect of your mortgage. Whether through scheduled meetings, phone calls or emails, we strive to be accessible and responsive. This ongoing communication ensures that you never feel alone in managing your mortgage and that you have an adviser to guide you through any financial decisions related to your home loan. Compare this option vs going direct to a lender (without the support of a mortgage broker) and wasting many

> This ongoing communication ensures that you never feel alone in managing your mortgage and that you have an adviser to guide you through any financial decisions related to your home loan.

precious hours on the phone, waiting in a call centre queue. Your choice!

By prioritising sustained support, regular reviews, proactive rate management, personalised financial guidance and open communication, the Ongoing Loan Adviser stage ensures that you receive continuous value and support throughout the life of your mortgage.

With 'The Brava Finance Way' four-step signature process, you can embark on your property purchase or refinance knowing that you have a dedicated and knowledgeable partner by your side every step of the way – aka your wing(wo)man! Don't let the perceived complexities of the process deter you from making a decision that may benefit your financial future. Let's work together to make your mortgage goals a reality.

In the next chapter, we'll explore one of the most important aspects of purchasing a property or choosing to refinance: how to prepare for a partnership with a new bank.

CHAPTER 5

SPEED DATE NIGHT

Preparing to partner with a new bank

Preparing for a new bank relationship, either due to a property purchase or refinancing, requires getting your documentation and information in order for the loan application process. Getting 'document-ready' ahead of time can provide time and effort benefits down the line.

In the first half of this chapter, I detail all the necessary documentation and information you'll need to gather and present to your new bank. Then, in the second half of the chapter, we look at the costs associated with starting a new banking relationship.

Getting document-ready

I won't sugarcoat it – this part of the process isn't exactly thrilling. But it's undeniably crucial. To ensure this process is as streamlined as possible, and to alleviate some of the associated headaches, my business uses a customer portal designed specifically for this purpose. With just a click, you'll gain access to your own section where you can input the necessary information and upload the required documents. It's a clear and user-friendly way to tackle this essential step.

So, what exactly do you need to gather? Let's break it down:

Identification

- Copies of your driver's licence and passport
- Most recent rates notice on all properties you own (if applicable)

Income

PAYG employment

- Two most recent payslips

- Most recent tax return

- Most recent notice of assessment (NOA)

Self-employed (sole trader)

- Two years of individual tax returns

- Two years of notice of assessments (NOA)

Self-employed (company/trust)

- Two years of company tax returns and financials

- Two years of individual tax returns

- Two years of notice of assessments (NOA)

- If you are buying in a trust, a copy of your trust deed is required

Rental income

- Three months of rental statements on any rental properties you own

Other income

- Documentation to support this income

Debt (outside mortgage loan)

- Three months of statements

Bank statements

- Six months of home loan history confirming balance and good conduct (if applicable)

- Three months of daily transaction history

- Three months of salary credits (if different from your everyday transaction account)

- Three months of savings statements

- Three months of statements for all non home-loan debts

At Brava Finance we use CashDeck as an alternative, and less time consuming, method for collecting bank statement data.

Personal particulars (questionnaire)

Included within the customer portal is a section to provide the following information required for the loan application:

- Three years of residential history

- Three years of employment history

- Assets and liabilities

- Monthly living expenses

- Needs analysis questionnaire – this is important to ensure any lender recommendation is within your best interests as part of the BID requirements.

Once we have received this information, the hard work is pretty much done!

We then use this information and follow a 'checks and balances' process to determine the viability of the application, most importantly:

- **Good conduct** – including on-time repayments, no overdrawn fees, no red flags (e.g. gambling)

- **Income** – confirming income amounts by checking pay slip and tax return information and/or company tax returns and financials

Included with the application is also your:

Once a lender has been determined, we will order a property valuation to ensure your LVR is less than 80%. Anything over 80% is determined as more risky by the lender, and it is more than likely that lenders mortgage insurance (LMI) will come into play.

- **Property valuation.** Once a lender has been determined, we will order a property valuation to ensure your LVR is less than 80%. Anything over 80% is determined as more risky by the lender, and it is more than likely that lenders mortgage insurance (LMI) will come into play. A property valuation is usually at no cost to the customer. You will be advised if there is a cost associated, depending on your lender choice.

> A property valuation is usually at no cost to the customer. You will be advised if there is a cost associated, depending on your lender choice.

- **Credit report.** Once your consent is received via the customer portal, we will organise a credit report to check that your credit score is within lender policy. If not, we may need to widen our lender search.

What I'm looking for

What am I, as your mortgage broker, looking for in all these documents? Allow me to explain…

Identification

This one is very simple. Forms of identification are used to prove you are who you say you are!

Bank statements

Here I am looking for evidence of good conduct. I look for salary credits to prove employment, and that your transactions are in line with your living expenses. I also look for any overdrawn account fees, evidence of debt not disclosed during the discovery stage (e.g. 'buy now, pay later' payments), red flags (e.g. gambling) and anything else that may happen to pop up. Any anomalies will need to be clarified with the customer and referenced in the broker notes supporting the loan application. Sometimes, too many red flags (e.g. a large number of overdrawn fees) may mean we cannot proceed with the loan application.

Payslips, tax returns, NOAs

If you are PAYG, I will use the information from the payslip to understand the breakdown of your pay (e.g. base/overtime/allowances) to determine the amount the lender will use for servicing. Some lenders 'shade' overtime (unless you're an essential service or medical worker), so the full 100% of the overtime pay cannot be used. I will also look at salary sacrificing, HELP debt payments and YTD amounts, which can be annualised, to get a better understanding of your pay. If the work isn't done at this stage, the wrong income figure may be used, which could impact servicing and viability of the loan application.

Self-employed financials

With self-employed applicants, it can be more difficult to determine income, and every lender is different in the way they treat this category. Some lenders use an average of the income recorded on the NOAs over a two-year period, some require net profit (plus addbacks) over a two-year period, and some lenders will look at one year of financials in isolation. This is another reason (if you needed one!) why it's so beneficial to use the services of a mortgage broker who understands different lender policies and niches and the best way to present your income depending on business performance history.

Personal particulars questionnaire

There is a questionnaire in the online customer portal that will need to be filled out before the application can be submitted. Best interest duty (BID) requirements state that any loan recommendation needs to be within the customer's best interests. So it is in this portal (and at the discovery stage) where these are documented and analysed to ensure the lender recommendation is in fact within your best interests.

Navigating the intricacies of the loan application process can be daunting, especially for first-time buyers or those with complex financial situations. That's where having a mortgage broker by your side can make all the difference. With our advice and guidance, you can navigate this process with more confidence, knowing that you have a dedicated ally in your corner every step of the way.

Navigating the intricacies of
the loan application process
can be daunting, especially
for first-time buyers or
those with complex financial
situations. That's where having
a mortgage broker by your side
can make all the difference

Fees and other expenses

As you navigate the mortgage landscape, it's essential to recognise that transitions in banking relationships can come with financial implications.

Whether you're wanting to purchase a property or refinance, the decision to break up with your existing bank and forge a new relationship requires careful consideration.

We will look at the various expenses and fees associated with both processes (property purchase and refinance), empowering you to make informed decisions. By understanding the potential costs involved, you can proactively manage your finances and ensure that your new banking relationship aligns with your long-term goals and aspirations.

Refinance costs

When weighing up the decision to refinance, it's essential to consider the associated costs within the broader financial picture. A good question to answer during your evaluation is how many months will it take for the potential monthly repayment savings to offset these costs? There are two typical cost categories associated with refinance: breaking up with your current bank, and starting a relationship with a new bank.

Breaking up

In the dynamic world of mortgages, 'breaking up' with your bank is akin to ending a long-term relationship and it can be a pivotal move towards a brighter financial future. Much like personal relationships, sometimes parting ways is the best decision to achieve your goals. It involves a process of weighing up the pros and cons – see a couple of the cons below:

- **Mortgage discharge fee:** The first part of the break up involves discharging your existing mortgage with your outgoing lender. This typically incurs a fee of around $350, although it's worth noting that some lenders may charge more or less. As your mortgage broker, I can access this information through my system and provide you with upfront details to avoid any surprises.

- **Fixed rate break fee:** If you currently have a fixed-rate loan with time remaining, you may also encounter a fixed rate break fee. This charge is imposed by the

In the dynamic world of mortgages, 'breaking up' with your bank is akin to ending a long-term relationship and it can be a pivotal move towards a brighter financial future.

lender and is calculated based on factors such as the loan amount, remaining fixed term, and changes in the cost of funds. While there are online calculators available to estimate this cost, your lender can also provide you with specific details upon request.

Starting a new relationship

Now, let's shift our focus to starting a relationship with your new bank. As with any new beginning, there are costs to consider, which should be disclosed early in the conversation. If you are using a mortgage broker to help with this process (and I recommend you do!), these costs may influence your decision regarding which lender to choose:

- **Set-up/application fee:** This can range anywhere from $0 to $600, depending on the lender and their fee schedule. A mortgage broker can provide you with a lender product comparison that compares different lender information, including set-up/ application fee.

- **Valuation fee:** This is typically priced between $100 and $400, although many lenders waive this fee altogether and absorb the cost themselves.

- **Monthly or annual account fee:** Some products may also come with a monthly or annual fee, particularly those bundled with package products featuring an offset account. Typically a basic home loan with redraw will not attract any monthly fees because the redraw is a feature of the home loan. But because an offset product is a separate transaction account (linked to your home loan) you are often charged for the additional account functionality, which includes a debit card for convenience.

> Typically a basic home loan with redraw will not attract any monthly fees because the redraw is a feature of the home loan.

- **Land registration fee:** Approximately $200. This is a fee charged to remove the old mortgage and replace it with the new home loan.

- **PEXA fee:** Approximately $50. PEXA stands for Property Exchange Australia and is Australia's online property exchange network. It enables users to lodge documents and complete financial settlements electronically. This fee covers the provision of PEXA's services, which includes setting up the PEXA file to facilitate communication with the outgoing lender for settlement date and time.

Property purchase costs

For many, buying a home marks a significant milestone, but it's essential to comprehend the financial commitments that come with it. From state-specific stamp duty to various administrative fees, navigating the costs associated with property acquisition is crucial for informed decision-making.

By understanding these expenses, you can proactively manage your finances and ensure that your dream of home ownership aligns with your long-term financial goals.

Stamp duty: Stamp duty (land transfer duty), is calculated as a percentage based on the property's value and varies between states. Understanding the applicable rates in your state is essential for accurate budgeting. You can use this calculator to work out approximate stamp duty costs depending on the state you live in: https://carajulian. com.au/mortgage-calculator/stamp-duty-calculator/. You may be eligible for exemptions and concessions from land transfer duty on your property, especially if you are buying

For many, buying a home marks
a significant milestone, but
it's essential to comprehend
the financial commitments
that come with it.

a home for the first time. You can contact your relevant state revenue office for more information.

Set-up/application fee: This can range from $0 to $600, depending on the lender and their fee schedule. A mortgage broker can provide you with a lender product comparison that compares different lender information, including set-up/application fee.

Transfer fees and registration fees: These fees encompass various administrative tasks, including mortgage registration and transfer of land, and are typically dependent on the property's value.

PEXA fee: Approximately $50. PEXA stands for Property Exchange Australia and is Australia's online property exchange network. It enables users to lodge documents and complete financial settlements electronically. This fee covers the provision of PEXA's services which includes the lender solicitor's charge for setting up the PEXA file to facilitate communication with the outgoing lender for settlement date and time.

Solicitor/conveyancer fee: Approximately $2,000. Engaging legal assistance during the property purchase process is crucial. Solicitors or conveyancers charge for their services, ensuring legal compliance and smooth transaction processes.

Valuation fee: Approximately $100 to $400. Typically, lenders will require their own valuation of the property and may expect the borrower to do this at their own cost.

Monthly or annual account fee: Some products may also come with a monthly or annual fee, particularly those bundled with package products featuring an offset account. Typically, a basic home loan with redraw will not attract any monthly fees because the redraw is a feature of the home loan. But because an offset product is a separate transaction account (linked to your home loan), you are often charged for the additional account functionality, which includes a debit card for convenience.

By understanding these expenses, you're better equipped to make informed choices that align with your financial objectives. Remember, transparency and foresight are key as you embark on any financial journey. With that in mind, let's proceed to Chapter 6, which pinpoints common mortgage mishaps, as well as tips that could help you pay off your mortgage faster.

Tips and tricks for your mortgage

In this chapter, we continue on our journey of navigating the complex landscape of home financing with more clarity and confidence. Understanding the nuances of mortgages is paramount, as it helps empower you to make informed decisions about one of the most significant investments of your life. In the first half of this chapter, we work through some proactive approaches to sidestepping the traps and pitfalls that can sometimes be encountered in the mortgage process. Then, in the second half of the chapter, we look at some key ways that may help you to pay off your mortgage faster.

20 mortgage pitfalls to avoid

From deciphering intricate terms to sidestepping potential financial hazards, this section is designed to help you navigate the mortgage world with more confidence.

Here are twenty common pitfalls to watch out for:

1. Ignoring upfront costs

As you discovered in the previous chapter, securing a mortgage loan often comes with fees and charges, such as mortgage discharge fees (in the case of refinance), application fees, valuation fees and legal fees. Failing to factor in these costs can have an impact on your financial situation.

As a reminder, here are some of the common costs (per loan) involved in a refinance (please note these are approximate figures):

- Mortgage discharge fee: approximately $350

- Set-up/application fee (not every lender charges a fee): This can range anywhere from $0 to $600.

- Title registration fee: approximately $200

- PEXA fee: approximately $50

And here are some of the common costs (per loan) involved in a property purchase (please note these are approximate figures):

- Stamp duty: This is calculated as a percentage based on the property's value and varies between states.

- Set-up/application fee (not every lender charges a fee): This can range anywhere from $0 to $600.

- Transfer fees and registration fees: These fees encompass various administrative tasks, including mortgage registration and transfer of land, typically dependent on the property's value.

- PEXA fee: approximately $50

- Solicitor/conveyancer fee: approximately $2,000

- Valuation fee: approximately $100 to $400

2. Focusing solely on interest rates

While interest rates are important, they shouldn't be the sole determinant for refinancing. Consider other aspects like loan terms, repayment options, product features and fees.

Failing to shop around and
compare different lenders and
loan products can result in
missing out on more favourable
mortgage options and finding
a lending solution that is
within your best interests.

3. Not assessing long-term costs

Particularly relevant to a refinance, spreading your loan out to a maximum 30-year loan term and lowering monthly payments may seem appealing, but extending the loan term can lead to paying more interest over time. Analyse the long-term costs before refinancing – or have your broker do this for you.

4. Inadequate research

Failing to shop around and compare different lenders and loan products can result in missing out on more favourable mortgage options and finding a lending solution that is within your best interests. You mitigate this by utilising the services of a mortgage broker!

Lenders generally require a certain amount of equity in your property to approve a refinance to satisfy their risk appetite.

5. Insufficient equity

Lenders generally require a certain amount of equity in your property to approve a refinance to satisfy their risk appetite. They consider a loan-to-value ratio (LVR) > 80% more risky, so may require you to pay lenders mortgage insurance (LMI). Remember that LVR is calculated by dividing the loan amount by the lender-assessed value of the property – expressed as a percentage.

6. Poor credit history

Your credit history and score play a significant role in refinancing. If your credit has deteriorated since taking out the original loan, it may impact your ability to refinance or result in less favourable loan terms.

7. Not considering your future plans

Refinancing may not be suitable if you plan to sell your property or make significant changes in the near future. Assess how refinancing aligns with your long-term goals.

8. Falling for teaser/intro/honeymoon rates

Some smaller lenders may offer attractive introductory rates that could potentially increase significantly over time. Ensure you understand the terms and potential rate changes before committing to a refinance.

Ensure that refinancing aligns with your overall financial goals and capabilities. Taking on more debt or extending the loan term may not be advisable for everyone.

9. Overlooking exit fees

Check if your existing loan has any exit fees or early repayment penalties – particularly if you are on a fixed rate. These fees can eat into the potential benefits from refinancing.

10. Neglecting to read the fine print

Thoroughly review all the terms and conditions of the new loan to avoid surprises, and ensure you understand the implications. Or you can have your mortgage broker walk through this with you.

11. Relying solely on online calculators

While online calculators can provide estimates, they may not consider all the variables. Consult with a mortgage broker or financial adviser for a more accurate assessment.

12. Not considering your financial situation

Ensure that refinancing aligns with your overall financial goals and capabilities. Taking on more debt or extending the loan term may not be advisable for everyone.

13. Omitting documentation requirements

Be prepared to provide all necessary documentation, including income verification and bank statements, to avoid delays in the refinance process.

14. Neglecting to factor in potential economic changes

Interest rates and market conditions can change over time. Consider how potential economic shifts may impact your refinanced loan in the future.

15. Forgetting about mortgage insurance in your calculations

If your loan-to-value ratio (LVR) is above a certain threshold (80% in most instances), you may be required to pay lenders mortgage insurance (LMI) on the new loan, which can add significant costs.

16. Not seeking professional advice

Consulting with a mortgage broker or financial adviser can help you navigate the refinancing process, understand the implications, and identify potential pitfalls.

Keeping on top of your budget
is key as you don't want any
surprises along the way!

---

17. Taking on unnecessary risks

Some refinancing options, such as switching from a fixed-rate to a variable-rate loan, may carry additional risks. Assess if the potential benefits outweigh the associated risks.

18. Rushing the decision-making process

Refinancing is a significant financial decision. Take the time to evaluate all options, crunch the numbers, and consider the potential long-term consequences before proceeding.

19. Not considering loan features

Different loan products offer various features like offset accounts or redraw facilities. Evaluate if these features align with your financial needs and goals as some features have higher rates and/or costs associated with them.

20. Not reassessing your budget

Keeping on top of your budget is key as you don't want any surprises along the way!

By understanding key concepts, leveraging professional advice and implementing proactive strategies, you can more confidently navigate the mortgage process and avoid common traps and pitfalls. Remember, a well-informed approach is the cornerstone of securing a mortgage that not only meets your current needs, but also aligns with your long-term financial aspirations.

Remember, a well-informed approach is the cornerstone of securing a mortgage that not only meets your current needs, but also aligns with your long-term financial aspirations.

6 reasons to pay off your mortgage early

Paying down your mortgage ahead of schedule is a goal that many homeowners aspire to. In this section, we delve into the significance of accelerating your home loan repayment. Then, in the next section, we explore six effective methods that may help you achieve this objective.

1. Interest savings

The longer you take to repay your mortgage, the more interest accrues over time. By paying it off early, you may significantly reduce the amount of interest you pay over the life of the loan.

2. Financial freedom

A mortgage-free existence can offer many benefits, including the potential for increased cashflow once the mortgage is paid off and you no longer have mortgage repayments to factor into your budget. This financial flexibility may enable you to pursue other ventures or

Home equity is a valuable asset that can potentially serve as a safety net during emergencies or be leveraged for other investment opportunities.

invest in your future. It would be worth speaking to a financial professional for more advice in regards to this.

3. Peace of mind

Owning your home outright can potentially alleviate the stress associated with mortgage debt. The threat of foreclosure or the risk of losing your home during challenging times can weigh heavily on some people.

4. Building equity

Home equity is a valuable asset that can potentially serve as a safety net during emergencies or be leveraged for other investment opportunities.

5. Retirement planning

A mortgage-free retirement can provide opportunities to allocate more funds to your retirement savings, which potentially results in a more comfortable post-work life.

A mortgage-free retirement can provide opportunities to allocate more funds to your retirement savings, which potentially results in a more comfortable post-work life.

6. Achieving life goals

Liberating yourself from mortgage debt has the potential to open up opportunities to pursue other dreams, whether it's travelling the world, starting a business, or supporting your children's education.

Consider switching from
monthly to fortnightly payments.
This strategy results in extra
payments each year, effectively
shortening the loan term
and reducing interest costs
over the life of the loan.

6 strategies that may help you achieve this

A mortgage represents a substantial financial commitment, but, with the right strategies, you can potentially liberate yourself from the burden of monthly payments sooner than you might think. Here are six strategies that may help you achieve early loan repayment.

1. Switch to fortnightly payments

Consider switching from monthly to fortnightly payments. This strategy results in extra payments each year, effectively shortening the loan term and reducing interest costs over the life of the loan.

2. Make lump-sum payments

Windfalls, tax refunds or unexpected financial gains can be directed towards making lump-sum payments on your mortgage. These additional payments can potentially reduce the principal balance and interest paid over time.

3. Refinance to a shorter-term loan

If you have room in your budget, refinancing to a shorter-term loan can accelerate your repayment schedule. While monthly payments may increase, the overall interest savings can be substantial.

4. Make extra payments

Whenever possible, allocate additional funds towards your principal balance. Even modest extra payments can compound over time, expediting the payoff process.

5. Cut unnecessary expenses

Review your monthly expenses and identify areas where you can trim unnecessary spending. Redirect the savings towards your mortgage payments to accelerate repayment.

6. Consider downsizing

If your current home exceeds your needs, downsizing to a smaller property could allow you to pay off your mortgage with the proceeds from the sale of the initial property.

Armed with these six strategies, you can start crafting a personalised plan to pay off your mortgage early. Begin by assessing your financial situation, setting clear objectives and establishing a budget (all outlined in Chapter 2, if you need a refresher). Determine the amount you can comfortably allocate towards your mortgage each month and implement one or more of the tactics outlined in this section.

Remember, paying off your mortgage ahead of schedule demands discipline and commitment. However, the long-term rewards far outweigh the effort invested. Envision the freedom of a mortgage-free existence and the many opportunities that may await you once you can attain this significant financial milestone.

While the journey to a debt-free life may pose challenges, with determination and prudent financial decisions, you'll be well on your way to owning your home outright, potentially securing a brighter future for yourself and your loved ones.

In the final chapter, I share some incredible success stories of women who have taken control of their financial narrative, albeit in different ways.

CHAPTER 7

Happily ever after

To the women forging their paths and shaping their destinies, this chapter is dedicated to you. Here, we celebrate three remarkable stories of female empowerment and home ownership, showcasing how women across generations have embraced the power of independence and financial freedom. Let's raise a glass to honour the resilience and strength of these women who have turned their home ownership dreams into reality.

Maddi, 28, first home buyer

Congrats on adulting so hard! How did it feel when you signed the papers and officially became a home owner?

Pretty shocked! I bought the house at an auction so it was pretty stressful and fast paced. I didn't expect to win this place at all as I had been looking at past auction results for similar style properties in the area which had gone way over the reserve price so I wasn't confident that I would win. During the auction I was already thinking about my backup plan.

What sparked your motivation to dive into the world of real estate at such a young age?

I was needing to move out of my shared rental and couldn't face going through the process again. I had been living in a shared environment for a while and was over it. Lots of my friends were buying their own homes so I started looking at what was available. Next minute I had engaged a real estate agent and a mortgage broker, and the wheels were set in motion. It also felt like the right thing to do. I wanted the security of having my own place; I didn't want to have to worry about rent increases, lease expirations,

It has always been about establishing the things of value to me. It's not about *not* spending any money, but finding things I want to spend money on. I didn't want to feel guilty spending money.

sharing with other people, etc. I wanted to be able to hang a shelf myself without calling a landlord for permission! Seemed like the right thing to do.

Buying a house is a big financial leap. Can you share the savvy strategies or financial tips that helped you make this significant purchase?

I was lucky to have had the influence of financially savvy parents growing up, so I have always been good at saving money, even as a little kid. I remember at a young age having a CommBank account and a little red pouch I would put my savings into, then pop along to the bank to deposit my money. It was a good feeling! Having financially savvy parents has also been super helpful as I have grown older. It is comforting knowing I have them as my support team to discuss my options with.

It has always been about establishing the things of value to me. It's not about *not* spending any money, but finding things I want to spend money on. I didn't want to feel guilty spending money. At times when saving was hard, I had to adjust my priorities. To keep me on track, I would often take a minute and weigh up all my other needs and wants versus having a house. I made choices to allow me to save money – I didn't have a car and I lived with my parents right through uni. So I had a good base. I worked hard and focused on saving money. I invested my savings into shares so I couldn't touch it until I was ready to buy a property. This helped my mindset a lot as I felt I had a good plan in place and was taking necessary actions to meet my financial goals while passively earning a wee bit of income. It felt good when I started looking at property knowing that I had this money sitting there.

Home ownership often involves unexpected expenses. How did you prepare for potential financial curveballs, and any advice for others on building a solid financial safety net?

As much as I hate to admit it, I wasn't as prepared as I should've been. My advice is to give yourself a safety net and be prepared for the unexpected expenses. When I first moved into my new place I discovered that the oven didn't work, plus I was hit with body corporate fees earlier than I had anticipated. I only just scraped through and it was a stressful time!

Investing in real estate at a young age is impressive. Were there any doubters or naysayers along the way,

and how did you prove them wrong with your financial prowess?

I was lucky that everyone was pretty supportive. However, some people were surprised that I did it on my own, without a partner. It is harder with only one income and I had to adjust my expectations, but I did it. I feel proud. I also love the financial freedom and security this gives me. Sometimes relationships don't work out, and things can become messy if you share a property together. Fortunately this is something I now don't have to worry about.

> Some people were surprised that I did it on my own, without a partner.

They say patience is a virtue. How did you stay patient and focused on your financial goals during the sometimes lengthy home-buying process?

I was pretty stressed during the process – and also very impatient. But I was lucky to have a great support structure around me of my parents and friends (including a real estate agent). I also found having a mortgage broker in my court was a huge help. I asked a lot of questions along the way to help build my knowledge and confidence. I spent the time reading through all of the information and documents to ensure I understood everything, which helped me feel more in control of the process.

In the world of real estate, knowledge is your secret weapon. Any books, podcasts or courses that you'd recommend to fellow aspiring young homeowners?

Google! I spent many hours googling anything I didn't know, which was a great resource.

You've officially levelled up in the real estate game. What's the next financial milestone you're eyeing, and how does home ownership fit into your larger financial strategy?

I feel like I need a break from my strict savings regime and would love to go on holidays for my thirtieth! This will be my savings focus for the next wee while. My medium-term plan is to stay in this place for the next five years and pay off as much of the loan as I can. Then I want to rent this place and use the equity to scale up to a bigger place to move into to meet my financial and personal goals.

In my industry (construction), I deal with a lot of men and have always found myself taking on the role of calming them down and managing their egos. I didn't realise how much that had taken over in my personality until I started this process.

Let's talk about celebrating victories. How did you commemorate the moment when you officially became a home owner with your finances intact?

Champagne!

Now that you've conquered the real estate realm, what financial advice would you give to other young women dreaming of making their mark in the home ownership arena?

It is doable. It feels daunting and I felt very out of my depth when I first started. Also to stand up for yourself during the process. At first I tried to pacify people and felt the need to please them. An example of this is with a couple of real estate agents I dealt with early on who were quite pushy. At the start I was trying to make them feel good for finding a property for me, telling them I liked it when I didn't. But by the end of the process and as my confidence grew, I would give my honest opinion without fear of how it would be received. Another example is at the auction for

> It is doable. It feels daunting and I felt very out of my depth when I first started.

the property I have just purchased, I increased a bid by $1,000. The auctioneer pushed it to $2,000 and moved on to sourcing the next bid. I pulled him up on it and ensured he took my $1,000 bid.

Building a good support team is key.

In my industry (construction), I deal with a lot of men and have always found myself taking on the role of calming them down and managing their egos. I didn't realise how much that had taken over in my personality until I started this process.

What's your favourite room in the new house, and why? Any quirky details that make it uniquely yours?

I love the living room. I have always lived in share houses so my bedroom was my only real private space. My new living room has a beautiful fireplace and mantel, and I have been able to decorate it how I like it – thanks for the mirror, Mum!

They say the kitchen is the heart of the home. What's the first meal you cooked in your new digs to officially break it in?

I haven't cooked anything yet as the broken oven is an ongoing saga. I bought the wrong oven! I am now waiting on a new one to be delivered and also finish some electrical work that needs to be done. I love baking so am looking forward to being able to bake my first cake in my new oven.

Share a funny story about the first time you met your new neighbours. Any memorable icebreaker moments?

The property I bought is quite old so it doesn't have any setback laws you see in modern buildings. For example, you don't normally have windows overlooking other houses' rooms. My bedroom has beautiful light and fabulous Art Deco features, and I love hanging out in there. The only issue is that it looks directly into the neighbour's bedroom. That first awkward wave through the window is definitely a memorable moment.

Let's talk about home dreams. If money and practicality were no issue, what crazy item or feature would you add to your new place?

I would love to knock out the dividing wall between the kitchen and dining room to create more of an open space.

Lastly, if your new house had a personality, what would it be, and how does it reflect your own awesome personality?

She is old but well looked after. A refined lady. There is a lot of personality and beautiful Art Deco features on the ceiling. I can't wait to do more styling – introducing colourful and vibrant features to tie in with the Art Deco style, which is a nod to my personality.

Liz, 32, married with separate finances

Can you briefly introduce yourself and tell us about your background?

My name is Liz, I'm turning thirty-two this year and got married in October 2022. I've been with my husband for eight years now. We met while I was completing my master's degree. I was working for seven years before quitting my job to start my own business this year.

How did you become interested in managing your finances independently, especially within the context of marriage?

My husband and I have always kept our finances separate. In the very early days, he took me out on a few dates, but since then we have split the costs of everything evenly. It just seemed like the easiest thing to do, as we didn't want to be affected by each other's spending habits and didn't want to argue about money. Also, as a side bonus, gifts feel a little more meaningful when you know you're not paying for half your own gift.

We each pay for our own individual expenses, and shared expenses like groceries, rent and bills are split 50/50.

Can you share some of the challenges you faced (if any) when initially trying to manage your finances independently?

I've never really faced any challenges with managing my finances independently as we have done this from the beginning of our relationship. I think the difference here is that when couples get together, at some point they tend to decide to open a joint bank account, or decide who will cover what cost. We never did that. We each pay for our own individual expenses, and shared expenses like groceries, rent and bills are split 50/50.

Were there any resources or tools that were particularly helpful to you in managing your finances, or were you already competent in this area?

I was already competent in this area. Actually, I feel like managing finances comes more naturally to me than it does to my husband as we were raised differently. My family had always run their own businesses, so we talked about money a lot, whereas money was more of a taboo topic in my husband's family, as it is with a lot of families.

How do you and your spouse approach financial discussions and decision-making?

Although we keep our finances separate, we discuss it all the time as we are very much a team and use the discussions as an opportunity to work out how to improve our individual financial situations together. I also personally enjoy these conversations as I find it interesting and there are not many people you can talk openly with about it. Like everything else, we approach financial discussions by discussing everything thoroughly and we normally wind up agreeing on everything as we have similar goals.

Given that I was taught more about finances from my parents, my husband has adopted a very similar mindset to mine when it comes to money. His relationship with money has changed a lot since meeting me. At the same time, I have

> Given that I was taught more about finances from my parents, my husband has adopted a very similar mindset to mine when it comes to money.

also learned from his point of view and the way I think about money has changed a little accordingly. I feel like I used to be too tight with my money and would force

So far I have bought two
investment properties
on my own.

myself to save it all, but now I make sure to live my life while saving responsibly! Overall we are currently very much on the same page when it comes to how we like to budget and how much we like to spend on things.

Can you share a specific financial goal you've achieved by managing your finances independently?

So far I have bought two investment properties on my own. I have accumulated a fair bit of equity now so I would have been able to buy more by now, but I have to put a pause on buying property as I am no longer on PAYG (pay as you go employee).

How do you prioritise your financial goals and make decisions about spending, saving and investing?

This has changed since starting a business and I am still navigating through this, but, as a rule of thumb, my approach is to generally be reasonable with my spending, then whatever is left over goes into my savings. I don't have a budget – I just don't spend money on things that I feel aren't worth it and I tend to not develop expensive habits such as eating out daily, so generally speaking I do have quite a bit left to go into my savings. This way of thinking has been ingrained in me since childhood. And then when I have enough, the plan is to invest in more property!

What advice would you give to other women who want to take control of their finances within their marriage?

> Just give it a go. It's not hard at all.

Just give it a go. It's not hard at all. I'm sure you were managing your finances by yourself at some point. It's also important to do this.

Have you encountered any misconceptions or stereotypes about women managing finances independently? How do you address them?

No, mostly because most people are not comfortable talking about money, and the ones who are have no problem with women managing finances independently. When I tell people that I manage my finances separately, I get met with one of two responses. Either people tell me something along the lines of, 'Oh, well, my husband and I have a joint account – we've been doing this since we bought a house together,' or they tell me that it's great that I do this.

How has managing your finances independently impacted your relationship with your spouse?

I think it has had a positive impact on our relationship. We help each other out financially if ever needed and we help each other to improve our financial situations. I also think it helps that our spending doesn't impact each other. There are things he buys that I wouldn't deem worth spending money on and there are things I spend money on that he would feel are unnecessary, but, since it's our own money, it doesn't bother the other party.

What role does financial literacy and education play in your approach to managing finances?

I think it plays a huge role in our approach to managing finances. As I mentioned earlier, my in-laws did not provide any financial education to my husband, so he has had to start from scratch, whereas I am grateful to have been given a strong foundation since childhood. My sister and I have recently talked about the fact that we are lucky to have this, because we've realised over the years that some of our friends make really bad financial decisions due to not knowing how to approach their finances.

Are there any financial mistakes you've made along the way? How did you learn from them?

Not really. I feel like I am generally very conservative.

How do you stay informed about financial trends, changes and opportunities?

I follow finance influencers on Instagram.

Can you share a personal finance tip or strategy that has been particularly effective for you?

If someone feels like they are spending too much and need to cut back, I would suggest for them to take a step back and review their spending. It's probably easiest to cut back on things that cost the most as this will have the biggest impact. And don't take an all or nothing approach as it is not sustainable. If you eat out for lunch and dinner every day, you can try cooking at home three days per week and slowly increase it instead of jumping into eating at home every day. I feel like mindset also matters. If you want to cut back on eating out, don't see it as a horrible

It means I'm in control of my money, and not the other way around. I choose to work because I enjoy what I do, which is different from showing up at a job you hate every day because you have to pay rent.

thing you *have* to do – put a positive spin on cooking at home and learn some fun recipes that you enjoy cooking and eating! Also, just little things like checking that you are getting a reasonable deal with insurance and utility providers – this will all add up.

What financial goals are you currently working towards?

I am currently rentvesting so I'd like to buy more investment properties and perhaps buy a house in Melbourne one day.

How do you celebrate financial milestones or achievements with your family?

When I buy a new property or if anyone in the family gets a pay rise or promotion, we tell each other and congratulate one another.

What does financial independence mean to you, and how do you define it in your own life?

It means I'm in control of my money, and not the other way around. I choose to work because I enjoy what I do, which is different from showing up at a job you hate every day because you have to pay rent.

Finally, what message would you like to convey to women about the importance of financial independence and empowerment?

Money is a personal thing, so you should really, at the very minimum, have a clear overview of what's happening with yours. Financial independence is so important, and it's really not hard.

> Financial independence is so important, and it's really not hard.

Linda, 50, single mum of two

So, you've been on a financial rollercoaster. Can you share a bit about the wild ride?

After separating from my ex-husband, I was shocked about how financially vulnerable I felt. Although I had a good understanding of financials, and my own business to provide income, I was all of a sudden in my own boat, needing to navigate my future financial security for myself and two young children. I had lost the captain!

If your financial journey had a theme song, what would it be and why?

'Under Pressure' by Queen and David Bowie describes exactly how I felt after coming out of my separation and realising that my financial security rested solely on my shoulders.

What's the most outrageous money-saving hack you swear by?

It's not outrageous but I did attend some Bunnings home DIY repairs courses that covered basic home maintenance

Trying to do everything all at once is overwhelming. The best way to approach it is to just have the courage to take the first step … and then the next … and confidence will grow tasks so I could avoid costly professional services for minor repairs around my house.

We've all got that one guilty spending pleasure. What's yours, and how did you make peace with it on your journey to financial success?

I like to get my nails done and I did reassess this 'luxury' when I redid my budget as a single mum, but I decided to allow for this in my budget because I prioritise self-care and this was an example of something that gave me a break and helped me feel good about myself.

If you could time-travel and give your younger self some advice on going through a divorce and getting back on your feet financially, what would it be?

Trying to do everything all at once is overwhelming. The best way to approach it is to just have the courage to take the first step … and then the next … and confidence will grow. Reach out for support from your friends and family, and gather a good support team of advisers to rely upon. To give you a game plan to follow.

Let's talk about the power of persistence. What kept you going when the financial road got bumpy?

My kids, and knowing that I had to keep going to create a financially secure future for us.

Money mistakes are like exes – we've all got them. Which 'financial ex' would you say taught you the most valuable lesson?

Trust your gut. If something doesn't feel right, it's probably because it isn't! I wasn't comfortable investing in the stock market because I didn't know much about it. I

> Trust your gut. If something doesn't feel right, it's probably because it isn't!

took some advice from a friend and invested some money and I actually lost money! Fortunately it wasn't a lot as I just wanted to dip my toes in, but it taught me a good lesson. I have since educated myself on stocks and don't feel like I am going in with my eyes closed anymore.

I spent a period of time out of the workforce as a stay-at-home mum and found that even after only a short period of time, my financial confidence started to take a dive.

Divorce is a tough journey. What financial strategies or lessons did you learn along the way that helped you rebuild and buy your own place?

I invested in educating myself in key areas that I felt I wasn't overly strong in. And with the help of professional advisers, I felt more confident navigating the 'financial world' journey.

Budgeting is a superpower. What budgeting hacks or financial habits did you adopt to ensure you were on the path to home ownership post-divorce?

I decided to keep it simple and created a simple spreadsheet, which tracked my spendings versus income so I could see the areas I needed to cut back on and opportunities for savings.

Did the gender financial gap play a part in your confidence after your divorce?

I spent a period of time out of the workforce as a stay-at-home mum and found that even after only a short period of time, my financial confidence started to take a dive. So it was during this time that I started my own business to increase my financial independence and start adding to my superannuation balance while still being able to have the flexibility to be with my children.

Did you have any outdated and archaic views of finances you brought into your marriage that played a part in your degree of financial confidence after your divorce?

Yes, while I was fairly well financially educated, I was inclined to rely on my husband during our marriage to make the financial decisions – especially after my first child was born and I became a stay-at-home mum. This was a big reason I felt so financially vulnerable after the separation because I was out of practice!

What financial adjustments or changes did you make in your lifestyle to pave the way for home ownership post-divorce?

I tightened the reins on my spending on non-essentials for the period I needed to save hard to build a deposit for a house. It wasn't easy. However, I kept my eye on the prize of home ownership, which I knew would create financial stability for my boys and myself. I even wrote myself reminder notes and put them up around the house, which helped a lot. There were definitely times when this became tough and all of my friends were going away on fancy trips, but I knew I had to keep focused on my goal.

Investing in oneself is key. What personal and financial growth did you experience that ultimately contributed to your ability to buy a house independently?

I did an awful lot of self-development work (once my head was in a position to focus!) to try and help the healing process. This helped create a more positive mindset, which ultimately made achieving more goals easier. Don't get me wrong – it wasn't always a straight-line trajectory. There were times when I felt I was going backwards!

Let's talk empowerment. How did the act of buying your own home contribute to your sense of financial independence, confidence and empowerment?

I remember the day my house settled and popping that bottle of champagne. I chose to celebrate on my own because I wanted the time to reflect on my journey and see how far I had come … on my own! I realised I didn't need my husband to create financial security. That was a huge uncovering and helped my confidence enormously.

Divorce can sometimes lead to financial surprises. Any advice on how to financially prepare for unexpected twists and turns on the road to rebuilding after divorce?

> One of the biggest ways to mitigate any unexpected financial surprises is to know what is going on with your finances at all times

One of the biggest ways to mitigate any unexpected financial surprises is to know what is going on with your finances at all times. Especially if you are in a relationship, know your financial position – understand your budget and be 100% across any debts you share because you never know what is around the corner and when you could be expected to have to manage on your own. It is a hard enough time just going through a divorce, let alone needing to uncover your financial position and deal with any nasty surprises.

Let's chat about financial self-care. How did you take care of your financial well-being while navigating the emotional aftermath of divorce?

Investing in financial education to help build my confidence made me feel more in control of my situation.

What financial goals or dreams are you now pursuing?

I have managed to build enough equity in my home to start investing in property, which is exciting!

Lastly, what advice would you give to other women who have been through a divorce and are working towards financial independence and the dream of home ownership?

You will get there. It's not easy but believing in yourself, investing in financial education and self-development, and building a strong network of support around you can make all the difference.

Date, don't marry

Congratulations on reaching the end of this enlightening journey through the mortgage landscape! *Why You Should Date Your Bank, Not Marry Them* was written with a singular purpose: to empower you, the reader, with the knowledge and confidence to navigate the mortgage world with confidence and bravado.

Throughout this book, I've delved into the foundational aspects of mortgages, the transformative benefits of working with a mortgage broker, and the importance of maintaining a dynamic relationship with your bank. You've gained insights into the step-by-step processes of refinancing and property purchasing, and you've been equipped with tools that may help you avoid common pitfalls and pay off your mortgage early.

By embracing the 'date, don't marry' philosophy, you are encouraged to approach your banking relationships with a sense of curiosity, empowerment and control. This mindset will put you in good stead to secure the most competitive deals and services available, ensuring that you remain in the driver's seat of your financial journey.

The opportunities on offer

Exploring the ideas and strategies presented in this book offers opportunities for:

- **A fundamental shift in mindset:** This book encourages a shift in perspective by challenging the outdated notion that men are solely responsible for managing finances. It fosters a more inclusive and empowered approach to financial decision-making.

- **Increased financial literacy and confidence:** Equipped with knowledge and key insights, you should feel more confident to make decisions in line with your financial aspirations.

- **A deeper understanding of costs and potential savings:** By gaining a deeper understanding of mortgage costs and potential savings, as well as the potential advantages of engaging a mortgage broker, you'll be better positioned to manage your financial commitments.

- **Awareness of common pitfalls:** With increased awareness and understanding, you'll be better equipped to navigate the complexities and potential challenges often encountered in the mortgage process.

- **Early mortgage repayment:** The book introduces various methods that you may find useful in managing mortgage payments. These strategies are designed to help you optimise your mortgage repayment approach over time.

Remember, individual outcomes can vary based on a range of factors, including personal circumstances and market conditions. It's essential to seek personalised financial advice tailored to your specific situation to make informed decisions.

Remember, the path to financial
confidence and bravado is
a journey, not a destination.
It requires continuous
learning, adaptability, and
a proactive approach to
managing your finances.

What to think about now

As you reflect on the information presented in this book, it's crucial to consider your current financial situation, goals and aspirations. Take some time to:

- **Assess your financial goals:** What are your short-term and long-term financial objectives? How does home ownership fit into these goals?

- **Review your banking relationships:** Are you getting the most value from your current bank? Is it time to consider dating other banks or engaging a mortgage broker?

- **Create an action plan:** Based on the insights gained from this book, develop a step-by-step action plan to guide you through your mortgage journey.

Remember, the path to financial confidence and bravado is a journey, not a destination. It requires continuous learning, adaptability, and a proactive approach to managing your finances. By embracing the principles and strategies outlined in this book, you are well on your way to a more empowered financial future.

Thank you for embarking on this journey with me. Here's to your financial success and happiness!

Be Brave | Show Up | Have Fun!

About the author

Cara Julian is a well-respected mortgage broker in Australia with a unique and personal understanding of the financial challenges women face. Growing up in a culture where men managed the family's finances, she carried this mindset into adulthood, leading to low financial confidence and dependence on her partners.

During a separation, Cara felt the unsettling vulnerability that comes from financial dependence. This experience sparked her passion for empowering women to take control of their finances and navigate the mortgage process with confidence and bravado.

Driven by her commitment to gender equality in the financial world, Cara founded Brava Finance, a mission-driven business focused on financial education and empowerment for women. She ensures they have the support, tools and knowledge to make informed decisions about their mortgages and financial futures.

Cara's expertise and advocacy have made her a respected voice in the industry. She's a sought-after media contributor and public speaker. Her holistic approach combines free resources, workshops, webinars, and public events, reaching thousands of women across Australia. Whether recently separated and unsure where to start or simply looking to build wealth and financial independence, Cara's clients benefit from her tailored strategies and unwavering support.

There's nothing Cara loves more than celebrating her customers' successes. Her genuine passion for helping women achieve financial independence shines through in everything she does, ensuring every woman has the confidence and knowledge to Be Brave | Show Up | Have Fun!

For more information on working with Cara you can:

Email: cara@bravafinance.com.au

Book a call: calendly.com/bravafinance/30min

Visit: carajulian.com.au

Or you can connect with her via social media:

Linkedin:

linkedin.com/in/cara-julian-73207528/

Instagram

instagram.com/carajulianmortgagebroker

Facebook

facebook.com/carajulianmortgagebroker

YouTube

youtube.com/@carajulianmortgagebroker